LIFE IN ANCIENT GREECE

Camelot
EDITORA

DISCOVER OUR BOOKS
ACCESSING HERE!

President: Paulo Roberto Houch
MTB 0083982/SP

Editorial Coordination: Paola Houch
Art Coordination: Rubens Martim (cover)
Translation: Francine Cervato
English text review: Francine Oliveira
Text Editing: Ana Vasconcelos (ECO Editorial)
Layout: Patrícia Andrioli
Images: Shutterstock

The legal deposit was made.

International Data of Cataloging in Publication (CIP) according to ISBD

C1811	Camelot Editora Life in Ancient Greece / Camelot Editora. – Barueri : Camelot Editora, 2024. 128 p. ; 15,1cm x 23cm. Translation of: A Vida na Antiga Grécia ISBN: 978-65-6095-099-3 1. History. 2. Greece. I. Title.
2024-1269	CDD 938 CDU 94(38)

Elaborated by Vagner Rodolfo da Silva - CRB-8/9410

Rights reserved to
IBC — Instituto Brasileiro de Cultura LTDA
CNPJ 04.207.648/0001-94
Avenida Juruá, 762 — Alphaville Industrial
ZIP CODE: 06455-010 — Barueri/SP
www.editoraonline.com.br

SUMMARY

THE GREEK LEGACY

The democratic conception of government, the constitution of cities as we know them, the process of seeking reason, philosophy, medicine, the conception of aesthetics through art, geometric laws, theater… We could list pages and pages of legacies that Greek civilization left for the history of mankind – an exuberant cultural heritage that influenced Western thought, science, and the arts.

In this work, you will discover how it all began, from the formation of the Greek people through the evolution of the city-states and the actions of Socrates, Plato, and other philosophers. You will also see how the habits and characteristics of the Greek people were echoed in other territories over a long period of time.

Unravel the stories of deities, architecture, arts, theater, and many other aspects of this civilization that influenced the formation of the world as we know it today.

1

THE FORMATION OF THE GREEK PEOPLE

THE TRAJECTORY OF THE CIVILIZATIONS THAT WERE THE BASIS FOR THE ETHNIC COMPOSITION OF ANCIENT GREECE

Before getting to know the rich trajectory and apogee of Ancient Greece, the great constructions, and the political and philosophical leaders, it is essential to understand the origin and formation of the people who occupied the current Greek territory before Homer, Socrates, Plato, Aristotle, Themistocles, and Pericles, among many others, could mark the names eternally in history.

Thus, it can be stated that in Greece and its surroundings (in southeastern Europe, known as the Balkan Peninsula), there is evidence of more than 50 human settlements since the Paleolithic – also called the "Chipped Stone Age," a prehistoric period that started approximately 2.5 million years BC up to 10 thousand years BC. According to historians, the civilizations of the time had an economy based on hunting, gathering, fishing, and mining, in addition to the production of domestic equipment (bowls and vases) from wood and clay. Spatulas, knives, hammers, and other tools were produced with horns and bones. There is evidence that the people of the region practiced navigation, because of the intense communication between islands of the Magnesia Peninsula, in the Aegean Sea.

In the Mesolithic Period, which marked the transition between the Paleolithic and the Neolithic, the first records of housing made of stone appeared, in addition to cemeteries, but the local populations still preferred to protect themselves in caves. The use of vessels became more frequent in the search for goods, and it is known that there was a process of cultivating plants, as well as the domestication of animals – with emphasis on the raising of pigs. Hunting, gathering and fishing remained the basis of Greek societies. It is worth remembering that hooks, amulets, spoons, and blades were developed at that time. From the moment that men and women started dedicating themselves to agriculture and livestock, population growth was observed in some regions of the Balkan Peninsula, paving the way for the next phase of the evolution of the Greeks.

The Neolithic Period – or "Age of the Polished Stone," between 10,000 BC and 3,000 BC – recorded the first villages installed in coastal areas and inland, in plains or mountains near rivers and lakes. The purpose was to take advantage of the fertile land, in addition to water for human and animal supply. An interesting characteristic at that time was the beginning of the division of labor between men and women: men took care of security, hunting, and fishing, while women planted, harvested, and educated the children.

GREEK CIVILIZATIONS OF PREHISTORY

The supply of food made it possible to increase leisure time in mainland Greece. It should also be noted that the need to store agricultural products and seeds for cultivation led to the creation of ceramic pieces, which would come to be seen as decorative objects. With the expansion of cultural contacts and commercial networks, several Neolithic products started spreading throughout Europe.

Within the Neolithic, in the period called "Aceramic" (6,800 BC-6,500 BC), a small number of sites housed up to 100 people who inhabited underground oval huts, partially excavated in the earth, with clay floors. The economic aspects were based on agriculture (oats, wheat, barley, lentils, and peas), livestock (cattle, sheep, goats, pigs, and dogs), gathering (nuts, olives, and pistachios), hunting, and fishing.

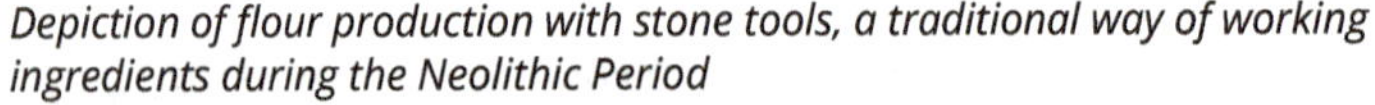

Depiction of flour production with stone tools, a traditional way of working ingredients during the Neolithic Period

Sculptures from the island of Delos, an important Greek archaeological site

The evolution of Neolithic people led to the formation of the Sesklo culture, one of the main cultures of Greek prehistory, with emphasis on the region of the same name, close to the city of Volos, in the central portion of the country. On-site, the wooden huts were replaced by stone huts, made up of bricks fixed with trunks intertwined horizontally and vertically. There were ditches to contain the water, wells to remove the liquid, and even a paved street. Sesklo presented itself as a walled village, covered by square and rectangular buildings.

Another civilization that expanded its influence in Greek prehistory was the Dimini, which prospered in the region of Thessaly (central-north area of the country). The settlements were characterized by large rectangular buildings and constructions made with stone (Dimini) or wood, as well as ditches and areas for specialized activities. In homes, in general, there were fireplaces and basements. Jewelry manufacturing, metal handling (silver and copper), production of marble figurines, trade, polyculture, and ceramics production represented the main economic activities of the settlement.

The Rachmani culture was the last Neolithic population on the Greek continental part, with records between 4,500 BC and 3,200 BC. Members preferred settlements in coastal areas, especially in caves, evidencing the importance of contact with the sea and commercial exchanges. Men and women evolved in cattle raising, and villages located in the lowlands became major economic centers during the period.

In the islands of the Greek territory, the highlight was Crete, the largest and most populous. The oldest evidence of the presence of human beings at the site are Neolithic ceramics from the remains of agricultural communities, dating from around 7,000 BC. The first inhabitants lived in caves. Gradually, they started forming small villages in addition to stone buildings. On the coast, there were fishermen's huts, while the fertile plains were heavily exploited. The people of Crete planted wheat and lentils, raised cattle and goats, and produced weapons with bones, horns, hematite, and limestone.

The civilizations of the Aegean Sea reached the Bronze Age with different degrees of evolution, but four of them stood out in the region of Greek territory. One group occupied the Cyclades region (an archipelago in southern Greece). The name, in Greek, means "circular" and indicates the more than 200 islands that are

Panorama of one of the islands that form the archipelago known as the Cyclades region

close to the island of Delos, which served, in Classical Antiquity, as a sanctuary for Apollo, venerated in Greek mythology as the god of the sun and the light.

In the Cyclades, the Grotta-Pelos culture was the first to be identified, developing between 3,100 BC and 2,650 BC. The buildings were rectangular, with up to two rooms with stone and clay walls. Settlements were small farming villages.

The Keros-Syros culture is characterized by a large number of small and short-lived settlements, in which each site, according to researchers, had a cemetery outside the walls of the fortifications. The buildings were erected with knowledge of masonry and had two floors. On Delos, smaller buildings were found, organized into rooms with rounded corners.

The group called Kastri also showed development in the Cyclades, between 2,400 BC and 2,200 BC, in the villages of Siros, Panormos, Delos and Keos. Tin, bronze, and silver work are important characteristics of the period.

The Phylakopi culture is considered the final phase of the people that integrated the Cycladic civilization. Large, well- organized villages started emerging. This population changed their preference for sites by the sea to fortified settlements in the interior of the islands, possibly due to the actions of pirates in the archipelago.

LIFE IN CRETE

The Bronze Age on the island of Crete began around 2,700 BC, with the introduction of copper for tools and weapons, marking the end of the Neolithic Period. The expansion of bronze use in the Aegean Sea is linked to population migrations on the coast of Asia Minor to Crete, the Cyclades, and southern Greece.

Such locations would begin a development phase marked mainly by the growth of trade relations with Asia Minor and Cyprus. With this, it is also observed changes in relation to the social organization, as well as technological improvements and a better quality of life for the inhabitants. Since then, the island has experienced a transition from an agricultural economy to more dynamic activities as a result of maritime trade with other regions of the Aegean and Mediterranean Sea. Crete came to occupy a prominent place in the area, mainly due to the fleet of vessels. Ports evolved into centers of influence, including trade with Asia. Villages were connected by

Village of Panormo, on the Greek island of Crete, a place that had representatives of the Kastri group

roads, and the access between regions became easier.

Also regarding the economic aspect, at that time, the inhabitants of the island already cultivated several species of cereals and vegetables, with an emphasis on the production of wine, grapes, oil, and olives. The technology linked to the use of animal traction was developed during this period.

Between 3,500 BC and 2,500 BC, the foundations were laid for the development of the Minoan civilization, one of the people that had the greatest influence on the consolidation of Ancient Greece and which originated in Crete.

POPULATIONS OF MAINLAND GREECE

The term "Helladic Civilization" is used to analyze a series of periods that characterized the culture of the Greek mainland during the Bronze Age. The classification encompasses people that lived in the region between 3,100 BC and 1,100 BC.

The Eutresis culture was the first to develop on the mainland. There are records of the group's activity between 3,100 BC and 2,650 BC, which built villages in Boeotia, Attica, Corinthia and Argolis.

Depiction of Minoan art in a palace at Knossos, on the island of Crete

The Korakou people were distributed throughout the Peloponnese Peninsula (southern Greece), Attica, Euboea, Boeotia, Phocis, Locris, and the island of Levkas, especially between 2,650 BC and 2,200 BC. Many settlements, especially in Argolis, were destroyed and burned before being abandoned or taken over by representatives of other cultures, mainly from the Mycenaean tradition, another population that exerted a strong influence on the Greeks.

The Lefkandi and Tiryns civilizations also showed outstanding development in regions of the Greek continental portion. According to experts, the Tiryns culture may be the result of a process of cultural integration between the Korakou and the Lefkandi, a "fusion" that occurred with different populations during the prehistoric era.

THE DEVELOPMENT OF THE MINOAN CIVILIZATION

The group comprising the Minoan Civilization flourished in Crete, especially after the introduction of copper, around 2,700 BC. The term "Minoan" was created by the English archaeologist Arthur Evans, who carried out excavations at Knossos, the largest archaeo-

Regarding clothing, fabrics were made from linen and wool fibers. There is also evidence of the use of silk, as silkworm cocoons were found. Women wore wide bell-shaped skirts with successive fabrics and elaborate decorative bands, embroidered sandals, high-heeled shoes, boots, jewelry made with precious metals and colored stones, eye and face coloring, as well as tattoos. Men wore clothes similar to those of shepherds and loincloths decorated with spiral designs, in addition to high boots.

Minoan plate with a depiction of the clothing of the civilization that occupied the region of Crete

logical site on the island. The name of the population derives from the name of the mythical king "Minos," who, in Greek mythology, was a semi-legendary ruler of the region, the son of Zeus and the Phoenician princess Europa.

In the Minoan hierarchy, kings were named after Minos, which would possibly have highlighted the origin of such a myth. In the epic poem "The Divine Comedy," by Italian writer Dante Alighieri, Minos appears as one of the judges of hell, hearing the confessions of the dead.

Minoan palaces are the best-finished constructions ever excavated on the island, as they served administrative purposes, based on large archives of documents unearthed by archaeologists. According to historians, the Minoan civilization was much more advanced than the contemporary Helladic civilization during the Bronze Age. According to research, the Crete occupied by the Minoan people remained free of invasions for many centuries and managed to develop a self-sustaining civilization, probably the most advanced in the

Minoan palace ruins at Knossos, in Greece

Mediterranean at that period.

The presence of specific works among the Minoans is an indication of high specialization, great workforce and successful division of tasks. A bureaucratic system and the need to control the circulation of goods formed the solid foundations for civilization, in addition to a possible economy based on a slave system. Over time, the power of the eastern centers begins to decline, being replaced by the influence of other localities.

The period between the 17th and 16th centuries BC represents the apogee of the Minoan Civilization, with administrative centers that controlled vast territories, as a result of the improvement and development of land and sea communications, as well as the construction of roads and ports. The presence of merchant ships was also fundamental, since they sailed with artistic and agricultural products, later exchanged for raw materials. Between 1,700 BC and 1,450 BC, the monarchy of Knossos conquered supremacy in Crete, with the system supported by the mercantile elite, creating a maritime commercial empire known as "Thalassocracy." The extent of the political system is proven by the large number of cities with the name "Minoa" found in the Aegean islands, on the Syrian coast, on the Greek mainland, and in Sicily.

The religion of the Minoan civilization was basically matriarchal, sustained mainly in the large number of female deities. In many images, there is a preponderance of depictions of women, including a "Mother Goddess" (of fertility) and a "Potnia" (lady of animals, protector of cities and families). They are depicted, for example, along with serpents and birds. The Minoans erected sanctuaries in natural places or in palaces. In addition, the mercantile elite possibly sustained their own authority through the ideology of kinship with the deities.

One of the currents of thought that tries to explain the decline of the Minoan people is linked to the volcanic eruption of Thera (or Santorini), which occurred in the Cyclades region between 1,650 BC and 1,450 BC, with a high level of destruction. The natural phenomenon devastated the Minoan settlement at Akrotiri, which was buried under layers of pumice. One group of scholars believes that the event seriously affected the civilization of Crete, although the exact extent of the impact is debated.

The first theories proposed that the fall of the ashes on the eastern half of Crete choked off plant life, causing starvation of the local population. There are hypotheses that noxious gases reached the island, intoxicating many living beings. In addition, the territory would have become a destination for refugees from the archipelagos of the Aegean Sea. As the Minoans were a maritime power and depended on the navy, the eruption created significant economic difficulties.

THE INFLUENCE OF THE MYCENAEAN PEOPLE

The Mycenaean Civilization is considered one of the most sophisticated societies of Greek culture because of its great artistic dissemination and advanced political organization, which, according to experts, advocated equality between men and women. It developed on the Greek mainland approximately between 1,600 BC and 1,050 BC. The term derives from "Mycenae," the name of one of the most important Mycenaean regional centers. Also called "Achaeans," they started their incursion into Greek territory around 2,000 BC, even conquering the inhabitants called Pelagius, natives of Greek territory.

The Mycenaean population was characterized by active trade. The group conquered the island of Crete around 1,450 BC. They exerted a notable economic and cultural influence in the region for 200 years. The people were characterized by an aristocracy of warriors and spoke an archaic form of the Greek language, Mycenaean Greek. The oldest documents in Greek were recorded by this civilization, which built fortified villages in Mycenae, Tiryns, and Pylos, among other important centers.

Several characteristics of Mycenaean culture survive in Greek religious traditions and literature of the Archaic and Classical periods, notably in the epopees "Iliad" and "Odyssey," written by Homer. Mycenae had its peak and was the most prosperous city in Greece for many years, influencing several sectors such as arts, engineering, and architecture.

In the evaluation of researchers, the Doric invasion (of the Dorian people) is considered the cause of the end of the Mycenaean civilization, marking the end of the Bronze Age. The Dorians concentrated on military activities and acted in war as a way to obtain resources. The Spartans were descendants of this civilization, a fact that explains, in part, Sparta's interest in battles during Antiquity.

HOMERIC PERIOD

In the study of Ancient Greece, the apogee of the Minoan, Mycenaean, Cycladic, and Helladic civilizations is also known as the Pre-Homeric Period (between 2,000 BC and 1,100 BC). It was a time for prominence of important people in the formation of the culture of the region.

The Greek population originates from ethnic groups that migrated to the Balkan Peninsula in several waves at the beginning of the second millennium BC: Achaeans, Ionians, Aeolians, and Dorians. The invaders are generally known as "Hellenics," whose organization of villages was based on the belief that the populations descended from the hero Helenus, son of Deucalion and Pyrrha.

The victory of the Achaeans (or Mycenaeans) in Crete, around 1,450 BC, opened doors to their hegemony in the eastern portion of the Mediterranean Sea. The domain was extended around 1,200 BC, when the city of Troy, in Turkey, was conquered, offering access to the lands of the Black Sea coast.

The Homeric Period (between 1,110 BC and 800 BC) is marked by the rise of city-state cells, Homer's epic literature, and the first written records using the Greek alphabet in the 8th century BC. According to archaeological records, there was a collapse of the civilization that inhabited the eastern Mediterranean world during this period. The great palaces and cities of the Mycenaeans were destroyed. Whole villages were abandoned. Such facts explain why this period of time is also known as the "Dark Ages."

According to historians, the Greeks lived in smaller dwellings, indicating a time of food scarcity and population decline. Gradually, monarchies started being replaced by aristocracies. In parallel, iron replaced bronze, which came to be used in the manufacture of tools and weapons. Family groups gathered around the so-called gentile community (or genos). In this type of social organization, the family was mobilized through the extensive exploration of agricultural activities. Each group had a patriarch responsible for dealing with several issues, with the work being carried out collectively.

With regard to writing, the use of the syllabic system of the Minoans (linear writing) fell into disuse, being replaced by the alphabetic system of Semitic writing, created by the Phoenicians. But it was by the Greeks that it started being used in other languages in the western Mediterranean. With that, the foundations for the dissemination of Greek and Homer's epic poems were consolidated.

2

FROM THE FIELD TO THE CITY-STATES

HOW GREEK IDENTITY WAS SHAPED FROM HOMER'S EPIC POEMS AND ORGANIZATION IN THE POLEIS

In the historical study of Ancient Greece, the Archaic Period (between 800 BC and 500 BC) was the sequence of the Homeric Period, in which the Greek population started grouping in the so- called gentile communities (the members of this social organization were also known as genos), characterized by self- sufficiency and the practice of agriculture. However, little by little, the genos stopped adopting the collective use of the land, the main asset of the time. In this way, a group of landowners started emerging. In most cases, the aristocratic class was closely linked to the patriarchal leader of these agglomerations.

The "eupatrids" (synonymous with "well-born") formed a group of aristocrats who started working for the maintenance of their own possessions. With that, the gentile community came to group into "phratries" and tribes controlled by the new aristocracy. In parallel, it was observed an increase in population, which has led to difficulties in accessing productive land.

SAILING IS NECESSARY

One of the solutions to the growth in the number of people was to bet on colonization and maritime trade. Those excluded from the land control process sought places with more suitable conditions. The migration of these people marked the so-called "Second Greek Diaspora," starting in 750 BC. This migration expanded the territories of the Greek world and created a trade network between the villages of the region.

The colonization consisted of detailed plans, with the appointment of the commander of the expedition (the "oikistes"), who would be responsible for the conquest of the territory and who would head the colony ("apoika" – in English, "distant residence"), as king or governor. Interestingly, before the expedition, the leader consulted the Oracle of Apollo on the island of Delphi, who approved the suggested location or proposed another one. In this way, Apollo was associated with colonization. Many colonies in Illyria, Thrace, Libya, and Palestine were named Apollonia in honor of the god. The colonizers took from the mother city, the metropolis, the sacred fire, and the cultural and political elements, such as the alphabet, the calendar, and the cults.

One of the first occupations of the period was carried out in 775 BC, an initiative of Greeks from the cities of Chalcis and Er-

In Ancient Greece, the word "tyrant" did not have the negative connotation applied today. At that time, the term meant "usurper with supreme power." Among the Greeks, the word only acquired a negative meaning after the government of the "Thirty Tyrants" in Athens (404 BC), known for adopting cruel practices against the population.

Bust of Periander, tyrant who ruled the city-state of Corinth and died around 585 BC.

etria, which left for the island of Ischia in the Gulf of Naples. It is also recorded, in the 8th century BC, the foundations of colonies in Sicily: Naxos and Messina (by Chalcis) and Syracuse (by Corinth).

CONQUEST OF COLONIES

The Black Sea coasts were mainly conquered by Miletus. The two most important colonies in the region were Sinope (700 BC) and Cyzicus (675 BC). The city of Byzantium was founded in 667 BC after a fleet left Megara. In the western region of the Mediterranean Sea, the occupations in Massalia (now Marseille) and Nice (from "Nike," which means victory), located in France, stand out.

One of the consequences of the colonization process was the development of trade relations. Until then, trade was not an economic activity in itself but worked as a support for agriculture. As a matter of curiosity, some cities, the emporiums, worked almost exclusively for the practice of trade but did not have any political status.

Alongside trade, industry started progressing more intensively. Thus, the production of ceramics, especially vases from

Corinth and Athens, became one of the main promoters of exports. According to historians, in the 7th century BC, the coin emerged in the region of Lydia (in the western portion of Asia Minor) and slowly started being used throughout Greek territory.

CHANGES IN THE SOCIAL ORGANIZATION

Power in the hands of the aristocracy – as well as the expansion of economic activities – offered the conditions for the consolidation of a fundamental space of representation in Ancient Greece: the city-state (or "polis"), which represented an urban core marked by political decisions and the circulation of goods.

Transformations in the economy and social organization of the Greek people produced significant changes in the way of life of the population. With the increasing arrival of products from the colonies and because of the importance that the export of wine and olive oil acquired, the idea of replacing the cultivation of wheat with vines and olive trees was developed among the higher classes.

Peasants with few economic resources were unable to carry out the replacement, as the vine and olive tree needed time to offer results; in this way, they would not be able to wait for profit. In addition, crops required less labor, causing some workers to be unemployed. As a result, it originated in the Archaic Period the class of "plutocrats," often born into lower classes, who became rich thanks to the progress of trade and industry, activities despised by the aristocracy.

The class had political ambitions, which, at the time, were related to land ownership. Thus, plutocrats and nobles, who did not intend to be relegated, also entered the race for land. The competition significantly affected peasants who had few resources. Their living conditions got worse.

Due to social instability, conflicts became more intense in the second half of the 7th century BC. Therefore, the city-states sought to peacefully resolve their conflicts. The disputing parties agreed to appoint legislators, men with "upstanding reputations," to establish codes of law and conduct in each region. Until then, the legislation was not written, which allowed arbitrary interpretations in favor of the aristocracy. It is noteworthy that the demand for a written code came from the popular classes.

LEGISLATORS AND TYRANTS

However, the production of legislators did not resolve social conflicts. Thus, between 670 BC and 510 BC, almost all Greek regions were under the rule of tyrants. They gained power through violence and received the support of the lower classes, who came to be protected. Tyrants took power, primarily, in the trading cities. The first known tyrants were Orthagoras in Sicyon and Cypselus in Corinth. The population of the city-state of Athens in the 6th century BC was ruled by the tyrants Pisistratus, and Syracuse by Dionysius the "Elder" and Dionysius the "Younger."

In general, tyrants were responsible for sharing land, the abolition of debt, and exemption from taxes. They also minted coins and launched public works, which would allow them to employ surplus labor. The descendants of rulers did not maintain support for the popular classes, and almost all disappeared before 500 BC, defeated by nobles or by the city-state of Sparta. Most tyrannies were succeeded by oligarchies or democracies.

MYTHOLOGY AND SPORT

The sacred grove Altis was located in front of Mount Cronus, between the confluences of the Alpheios and Kladeos rivers. According to mythology, it was in this place that Zeus defeated his own father, Cronus (god of time and lord of the sky).

The games had great importance for the Greeks since they had a religious, political, and sporting character. First, it was a way to honor the gods. It was also an important moment in the search for harmony among the city-states. The initiative served as an event to value health and the body.

Foreigners, slaves, and women could not participate in the games. The athletes were, in general, from the upper classes and had practiced the sport since childhood. They arrived not just from mainland Greece but from several parts of the Greek world, which, in antiquity, included the colonies scattered along the shores of the Mediterranean and Black Seas. The winners were honored in their places of origin; they could receive free food, have statues built, and be sung by poets.

OLYMPIC GAMES ORGANIZERS

The organization of the event was in charge of the polis of

Elis (in western Greece). In 668 BC, Phaedo of Argos, a Greek king who reigned between 675 BC and 655 BC, conquered Olympia and handed over control of the sanctuary to the city of Pisa (located in the Elis region), which organized the games until 558 BC, the year in which Elis retook control over Olympia thanks to the intervention of Sparta.

In the year in which the games were celebrated, Elis sent throughout Greece representatives who announced the exact date on which the competitions would be held and invited the athletes. Messengers disclosed the sacred truce. By rule, war was prohibited during the period, as it had the objective of protecting spectators and competitors during the trip, stay, and return.

The games were supervised by referees, known as Helanocides ("referees of the Hellenes"). The referees came from the nobles of Elis, being chosen ten months before the start of the festival. The referees should ensure the good condition of the sanctuary buildings, in addition to policing. They could interfere in disputes, raffling the competitors, arbitrating the tests, and proclaiming the winners, who were crowned. Athletes and coaches arrived at Elis a month in advance, to train under the supervision of the referees.

The outstanding Olympic competitions during the period were foot racing, equestrian racing, wrestling, pugilism (also called pugliato), pankration (a combination of wrestling and pugilism), and pentathlon. Over time, new modalities became part of the program, such as, for example, discus throwing, swimming, long jump, among others.

GAME EDITIONS

At first, the trials lasted one day, as only the stadium race was held. Only in 708 BC, in the 17th edition of the event, the competition started having two days, with the introduction of two modalities. In the 6th and 5th centuries BC, the games lasted five days.

On the first day, the athletes and referees took the oath, and the Olympic torch was lit. Fire was sacred and was associated with Greek religion, as almost every temple had a lit torch. After the opening ceremony and the oath, the games started in the morning.

On the evening of the second day, the first celebrations for the victors took place, with a feast and a ceremony. On the fol-

The core of Olympia was Altis, a sacred grove. In the center of the site, there was a Doric-style temple dedicated to Zeus, which was built between 468 BC and 456 BC. Inside, there was a giant statue of the god, by Phidias, and which was considered one of the Seven Wonders of the Ancient World.

Discobolus, a marble statue by the Greek sculptor Myron, depicts a discus thrower during an Olympic event

lowing day, in the morning, the traditional sacrifice of 100 bulls was carried out before the altar of Zeus, in the presence of all. The sacrificed animals would have parts highlighted as offerings. The rest would be prepared for a feast at night.

On the fourth day, the last trials were finalized. On the fifth day, all winners received laurel wreaths and red ribbons in the temple of Zeus. Then, the festivities began to celebrate the champions and the closing of the games. The following day, the delegations and visitors began their return trip.

The greatest period of the Olympic Games in Ancient Greece corresponded to the 5th century BC. Tensions related to the Peloponnesian War had a negative impact on the games as the city-state of Elis (which, until then, maintained a politically neutral attitude), allied with Athens, banished the Spartans.

PROTECTED ATHLETES

In 424 BC, for example, under the threat of invasion by Sparta, the games had to be held under the protection of troops. In 365 BC, Arcadia, helped by Pisa (an enemy of Elis), conquered the sanctuary; the two cities hosted the games of 364 B.C. Elis tried to recover the sanctuary by force; the conflict generated led to the assault and looting of the temples of Altis. Elis regained control of the sanctuary, and the games of 364 BC were declared invalid.

In the year 336 BC, several Greek cities were dominated by Philip II of Macedonia and his son, Alexander the Great. With that, the controllers of the territory built, in the sacred grove of Altis, the monument called "Philippeion," a building with statues of Alexander and his family, made of gold and ivory, materials that had been reserved for the sculptures of the gods.

The Romans conquered Greece in 146 BC. To finance wars, the Roman general Sulla looted the Altis grove (beyond the sanctuary at Delphi, in the Cyclades region). In 80 BC, as a way of celebrating the success of the battles, the commander transferred the games to Rome. After the general's death in 78 BC, the games returned to Olympia.

CONTROVERSIES REGARDING HOMER

Homer's period of existence was also the subject of controversy in antiquity. The Greek historian and geographer Herodotus said that Homer lived 400 years before his own time, which would place him around the year 850 BC. However, other ancient sources give dates closer to the time of the Trojan War, whose reference brings to the period between 1,194 BC and 1,184 BC, in reports by Eratosthenes (a Greek mathematician and poet of the 2nd century BC), who worked to establish a scientific chronology of events.

In addition to Homer's two major productions, the publications "Margites" (a comic poem about a clumsy hero), "Batrachomyomachia," a parody of the Iliad that tells of an incredible war between frogs and mice, and the so-called Homeric Hymns are attributed to him.

Before the beginning of philosophical thought, which would reach its peak in Ancient Greece with Socrates and Plato, Homer's outstanding works tended to bring the gods closer to men in a movement of rationalization of the divine, according to specialists. The Homeric gods, who lived on Mount Olympus, had characteristics that resembled those of human beings.

REVERENCE TO THE HOMERIC POEMS

In the same way as his birth, little is known about the poet's death. According to historical documents from the 5th century BC, Homer would have died on the Greek island of Ios in the Aegean Sea around 898 BC.

Regardless of the several doubts that surround Homer's life and work, the poetry constructed by him was highly revered throughout Antiquity, with verses considered a general source of wisdom. Almost all of Western literature was influenced to varying degrees and levels by the Homeric poems, through the work of countless writers.

THE TROY BATTLES

The battle of Troy, located in a province of Turkey, took place around 1,200 BC, when the Achaeans (one of the groups that formed the Greek people) attacked the city, trying to take revenge for the kidnapping of Helena, wife of the king of Sparta, Menelaus, brother of Agamemnon.

According to legend, the goddess of the sea, the nymph Thetis, was desired as a wife by the brothers Zeus and Poseidon. However, the Titan Prometheus (who had the gift of prophecy) prophesied that the son of the goddess would be greater than his father. Thus, the gods decided to offer Thetis as a wife to Peleus, an elderly mortal, planning to weaken her son, who would be human, with limitations. The warrior Achilles was born from this union, whose mother, trying to strengthen her son, dipped him in the waters of a river.

The waters made Achilles a powerful being, except for his heel, where his mother held him to dip him in the river. In this way, Achilles became the most powerful of the warriors, but he was still mortal. Later, Thetis prophesied that Achilles could choose between two fates: fight in Troy and achieve eternal glory, but die young, or remain in the homeland and live a long life, being quickly forgotten.

THE APPLE OF DISCORD

For the wedding of Peleus and Thetis, all the gods were

invited, except Eris, goddess of discord, who felt offended, attended the celebration invisible, and left a golden pome (a type of apple) with the inscription "for the most beautiful." The goddesses Hera, Athena, and Aphrodite competed for the pome and the title of the most beautiful. Zeus then ordered the Trojan prince Paris (at the time, being raised as a preacher) to settle the dispute.

To win the title of "the most beautiful," Athena offered Paris the leadership of a historic war. Hera (the goddess of marriage) presented the monarch with the glory of being the absolute king. Aphrodite (the goddess of love) would allow him the love of the most beautiful woman in the world. Paris gave the pome to Aphrodite, gaining protection but drawing the hatred of the other two goddesses against Troy. Aphrodite knew exactly who the most beautiful woman in the world was: Helena.

Aided by Aphrodite, the couple ran away to Troy. When he learned of the betrayal, Menelaus asked his brother, King Agamemnon, to help convince all the great generals and kings of Greece in a battle against the Trojans, including the sovereign of the province of Ithaca, Odysseus (in Latin, Ulysses), the architect of the plan with the Trojan Horse.

THE CONQUEST OF THE CITY

Agamemnon saw in his brother's misfortune the perfect opportunity to conquer Troy, until then known as impenetrable. From that moment on, the well-known war began.

The Greek ships landed on the beach near the city and started a siege that would last ten years, costing the lives of many warriors on both sides. Thus, following a trap proposed by Odysseus, the Greeks managed to invade the city ruled by Priam and end the war.

ADVENTURES OF ODYSSEUS

The poem, with 24 songs and 12,000 verses, recounts the return of Odysseus (Ulysses, as he was called in Roman myth), the hero of the Trojan War and the protagonist who gives the work its name. According to the plot, it took him ten years to reach his homeland, Ithaca, after the battles, which also lasted for a decade.

Several participants in the war had returned to Greece, but Odysseus was held back by a storm at sea, which diverted the commander's course. Meanwhile, his wife, Penelope, was courted by several suitors. According to tradition, since it was believed that Odysseus was dead, the widow should choose another husband. The dispute started.

With a daring strategy, Penelope deceived the suitors. She proposed to them that she would choose a suitor as soon as she finished weaving a shroud (a garment that involves the dead, who will be buried). She embroiders during the day but undoes the piece at night. As time goes by, the suitors ruin Odysseus' assets.

RETURNING HOME

Athena, the goddess of wisdom, hidden in the body of an outsider, encourages the couple's son, Telemachus, to look for his father. After overcoming several difficulties, he starts the search, while Odysseus experiences several adventures, also going through the land of the dead. The protagonist returned home with the help of some gods, but he did not reveal himself promptly. To defeat his opponents, he disguised himself as a beggar, following Athena's advice. Odysseus eliminated enemies because he carried a powerful bow. With the help of his son, he was finally recognized by his wife and his father. The island of Ithaca was at peace again, with the Odyssey completed.

ATHENIAN POLIS

The city of Athens is located in the center of the Attica plain, on the shores of the Aegean Sea. In the classical period, it presented an urban life and was open to novelties. The basis of the economy was commercial activity, based on the exchange of products with people from different territories.

Athenian society was dominated by the "eupatrids," who were great landowners. However, the power of this group was challenged by the lower orders and by the merchants, who demanded greater equality of rights. Small landowners were constantly threatened by debt slavery. Merchants, artisans, and urban workers, known as "demiurges," were excluded from political decisions and wanted to participate in them.

The result of these pressures was a legislative reform made

by Solon, an Athenian judge. From these alterations, debt slavery ceased to exist, and the right to vote was expanded, according to the assets each one owned.

However, Solon's reforms only benefited wealthy merchants. The rest of the population continued to be excluded from political decisions. The situation in Athens was tense. Furthermore, the city was dominated by the tyrant Pisistratus for more than three decades.

After the period of tyrannical governments, the person responsible for a new reform was Cleisthenes, an aristocrat concerned with the problems of the popular classes. He extended the right of political decision to all Athenian citizens – that is, all free men born in Athens over 18 years of age. The city was divided into "demos," a type of district that elected representatives to the assembly, which, in turn, chose the members of the council responsible for governing the polis. However, foreigners, women, and slaves were still excluded.

As for education, the Athenians believed that the city-state would be stronger if each boy fully developed the best skills. Education was neither free nor compulsory. The boys should already be going to school at the age of 6 and were under the supervision of a pedagogue, with whom they learned arithmetic, literature, music, writing, and physical education. Classes were interrupted on days of religious festivals and when students turned 18.

From then on, the boys were recruited by the government for military training, which lasted approximately two years. Athenian women performed domestic duties. Parents tried to quickly marry their adolescent daughters, who, after the nuptials, were under the control of their husbands.

THE CITY-STATE OF SPARTA

The Spartan polis was founded by the Dorians around the 9th century BC. The city was located in a region called Laconia, on the Peloponnese Peninsula. The area had mountainous and dry soil, which made the cultivation of supplies difficult. Such conditions led the Spartans to conquer fertile lands through wars. Power was exercised by a small group linked to military activities. A minority participated in political and administrative decisions, known as "Spartiates," who dedicated themselves solely and exclusively to politics and battles.

Life in Sparta revolved around war. The local inhabitants feared that the people they conquered would rebel, as well as being concerned about slave uprisings. The rulers prohibited travel and most trade contacts. In this way, Sparta closed itself off and imposed on its residents an authoritarian way of life and subordination to the interests of the state.

Agriculture, handicrafts, and trade were practiced by the so-called "Perioikoi," the free men, who did not have the right to participate in political aspects of the territory. Slaves were called "helots," who belonged to the state and worked for the Spartans. Young men were educated by the state. At the age of 7 they would leave their own homes and start to dedicate themselves to military training.

THE CITY OF CORINTH

In Ancient Greece, the polis of Corinth was a wealthy trade center, and it housed a cosmopolitan population, thanks to its port, located less than 50 kilometers from Athens. The local residents carried out a lucrative trade with Asia, in addition to establishing a point of communication with cities on the Italian Peninsula.

The site of the ancient city was already inhabited in the Neolithic Period (5,000 BC to 3,000 BC) and flourished as an important center in the 8th century BC, continuing with that characteristic until its destruction by the Romans in 146 BC. The polis was known as a naval power, which allowed ancient Corinth to establish colonies in Syracuse (on the island of Sicily) and in Corcyra (present-day Corfu, near Albania). The colonies served as trading posts for bronze ornaments, textiles, and ceramics produced in the metropolis.

From 582 BC on, Corinth started housing the Isthmian Games, celebrated in honor of Poseidon, the god of the sea. The Doric Temple of Apollo, one of the main landmarks of the city, was built in 550 BC, at the height of the city's wealth. The ancient polis was partially destroyed by the Romans in 146 BC, but in 44 BC it was rebuilt as a city of the Roman Empire. New Corinth prospered, and it is estimated that it had around 800,000 inhabitants at the time of the apostle Paul. It was the capital of Roman Greece, inhabited mainly by free men and Jews.

THE GREAT TROJAN HORSE

The Trojan Horse was a great wooden artifact used by the Greeks during the battles for the conquest of the fortified city, whose ruins are in Turkish lands. Taken by the Trojans as a symbol of victory, it was carried inside the walls without the Trojan warriors knowing that the enemies were inside the structure.

At night, the warriors got off the horse, dominated the watchmen and allowed the entry of the Greek army, which led to the city's ruin. In Homer's poems, the fact is briefly recorded in "Odyssey." In the centuries that followed, other writers expanded and detailed the episode.

In general, the horse is considered a mythic creation, but it is possible that it actually existed. It proved to be a fertile literary and artistic element, being, since antiquity, mentioned and reproduced several times in poems, novels, paintings, sculptures, monuments, movies, caricatures, and toys.

Replica of a Trojan Horse in the central square of Canakkale, Turkey, donated to the city after the filming of a movie

3

THE GREEKS AND THE WARS

HOW THE CITY-STATES OF ANCIENT GREECE FACED, IN POLITICAL AND MILITARY MATTERS, EXTERNAL AND INTERNAL THREATS

The Classic Period of Ancient Greece (between 500 BC and 338 BC) comprises a relatively short period, but it is marked by events of great importance that echoed in the following centuries in the Mediterranean region. Experts even evaluate that this interval represented the height of Greek civilization.

One of the main characteristics of the Archaic Period, the predecessor of the Classic, is the rise of city-states, based on a consolidated model of political decentralization and administrative independence. This meant that each region determined its own trajectory, with rulers who could make different decisions. For example, Sparta had an oligarchy focused mainly on military concerns. On the other hand, the Athenians verified the evolution of democracy through the action of the local aristocracy.

The strength of the city-states continued to grow, but amidst battles between the rulers themselves, which also had the participation of other people. Several clashes occurred in Greek territory, with emphasis on two of them: the Persian Wars (also known as Greco-Persian Wars) and the Peloponnesian War.

THE TENSION BETWEEN PERSIANS AND GREEKS

If in the internal environment the atmosphere was tense due to the differences between the Greek city-states, the external scenario presented the rise of the Persian Empire, especially after Cyrus II conquered the kingdom of the Medes – people who migrated from Central Asia to the Iranian Plateau, later known as Media. The monarch ruled between 559 BC and 530 BC, the year in which he died in battle.

The center of the empire was Persia, which stretched from Egypt to Pakistan. When the Persians invaded Asia Minor (now Turkey), the next step was to occupy Europe to control Greece. The Persian administration continued with a policy of expansion and occupied the Greek cities on the coast of Asia Minor, imposing defeats on the Ionians (one of the groups that formed the Greek population). What was at stake was the control of maritime trade in the region. It is noteworthy that most of the city-states in the north of the Greek peninsula surrendered without resistance. Each individual of the people subjected to the Persian Empire was considered a *"bandaka"* (slave of the monarch).

Athens and Eretria supported the uprising of Greek cities

against Persian rule, but the aid was insufficient. An example of this is the village of Miletus, which was taken and razed. In this way, so many Ionians decided to run away to the western colonies. Athens' behavior would generate a Persian reaction and was one of the factors that triggered the Persian Wars, recorded between 490 BC and 479 BC.

The battles began after Attica, on the Greek mainland, which includes the city of Athens, was occupied by the forces of the Persian emperor Darius I, who had already gone through and destroyed Eretria. The meeting between Athenians and Persians took place in the city of Marathon, about 40 kilometers away from Athens. According to historians, the monarch commanded around 50,000 men and, with a powerful navy, landed on the plain to repress the Athenians for their assistance during the Ionian rebellion.

The Athenian general Miltiades sent an appeal for help to the Spartans. However, they replied that they could only send the troops in a week, as they were amidst religious celebrations. Despite the denial, the general knew the Persian battle tactics and decided to move the troops to Marathon in order to face the invaders.

THE BATTLE OF MARATHON

According to historical records, the Battle of Marathon took place in September 490 BC. About 10,000 Greek fighters (who had the help of residents of a small town called Plataea) began the attack against the Persians, and they were looking for a hand-to-hand confrontation. They surrounded the opposing troops and threw themselves against the soldiers of Darius I. The Persians offered resistance and managed to break the Greek siege, which soon regrouped and won the conflict. Defeated troops returned to Asia. Persia's casualties were estimated to have reached 6,000. On the Greek side, the estimated number was around 200 deaths.

This was the first major confrontation between the two people. New clashes would occur and be decisive in defining the trajectory of both populations in the Aegean Sea region, following the Persian Wars.

Herodotus reports that Phidipedes was a "hemerodrome," the name given to official couriers who were able to cover large distances daily at a fast pace. A vigorous athlete and soldier, the professional runner worked as an army messenger. With the approach of the Persian army, before the battle of Marathon, the Athenians sent him to Sparta to seek help, covering a distance of more than 200 kilometers.

Herodotus reports that, during the journey to Sparta, the mythological god Pan (of flocks and shepherds) appeared to Pheidippides on a hill near the city of Tegea, on the Peloponnese Peninsula. Pan would have called the messenger in a loud voice and ordered him to ask the Athenians why he was not worshiped. The athlete said that the inhabitants of Athens would be immensely grateful if the god helped them against the Persians. According to the Greek literature, Pan sided with the Athenians at the Battle of Marathon. In gratitude, a place of worship was created for the god near the village of Tegea.

40-kilometer mark (approximate distance to Athens) located in the city of Marathon, Greece

DID YOU KNOW?

The origin of the athletics event known as "Marathon" refers to the battle won by the Greeks against the Persians. According to Greek literature, with references even to the geographer and historian Herodotus, a legendary Athenian runner called Phidipedes would have made the journey from Marathon to Athens to inform the residents of Athens about the victory over the forces of Darius I, running the stretch that corresponds to the modality that is part of the program of the Olympic Games.

It is said that, after the victory and expulsion of the invaders, enthusiastic about the feat, general Miltiades ordered Phidipedes to run once again to Athens, in order to inform the Greeks that the clashes were over. Shortly after announcing the victory, the messenger would have died due to exhaustion.

THE PERSIAN WARS CONTINUE

Commander of the Greek troops in Marathon, General Miltiades took advantage of the moment of glory to expand the power of Athens in the Aegean Sea. Thus, shortly after the battle in mainland Greece, the military sent a part of the fleet to fight in the archipelago of the Cyclades region, which was submitted to the power of the Persians.

The first move was an attack on the island of Paros, in which the Athenians demanded a large sum of tribute from the local inhabitants. The residents of Paros denied the payment, and the region was occupied. The resistance was great, and the only way out for the Greeks was to carry out looting. After the decision, the residents of Athens started becoming disillusioned with Miltiades, coming to see the general as a tyrant who depreciated the laws.

The commander's political enemies accused him of having deceived the people and submitted him to a trial, in which he was declared guilty. He was saved from the death penalty, which was a common procedure, on account of services rendered to the fatherland. However, the general was sentenced to pay a high fine. Shortly after, the general died due to wounds sustained in a battle. The political command of Athens would be in charge of Themistocles, who also had the military skills of a general and great power of persuasion over the city's residents.

In 481 BC, the representatives of several Greek poleis, led by Athens and Sparta, signed a military agreement to protect themselves from a probable attack by the Persian Empire. According to the pact, in case of invasion, Sparta would be responsible for commanding the Hellenic army in a general truce, which even made the return of political exiles easier.

THE SUCCESSOR OF DARIUS I

At the same time, in Persia, after the death of Darius I, his son, Xerxes I, rose to power. The monarch decided, in the early years of his reign, to repress uprisings in Egypt and Babylon, but he still continued to prepare to attack the Greeks. Earlier, the emperor sent ambassadors to the cities of Greece to ask the rulers for land and water, symbols of submission. Many municipalities and islands accepted. However, Athens and Sparta decided to resist, as well as other Greek regions. It would be the beginning of another Persian attack in the episode known as the Second Persian War.

The army of Xerxes I, estimated at up to 70,000 men, left for the invasion of the Greek territory in 480 BC. The troops marched and entered the Balkan Peninsula. The Greek fighters, who knew the enemy movements, decided to stop them in the gorge known as Thermopylae (in Greek, "hot doors"), in the continental portion, northwest of Athens.

In this place, the Spartan king Leonidas, who commanded the Greek forces, mobilized 300 soldiers from Sparta and approximately a thousand from other regions, in order to contain the Persian forces, who sent a notice in which they demanded the surrender of the reduced Hellenic troop. After five days of waiting and considering that numerical superiority did not intimidate the enemy, the Persians decided to attack.

According to historians, the gorge was so narrow that the military of Xerxes I could not use cavalry. In addition, the numerical superiority of the troops was blocked, as the narrow strip of land made the Persians reduce their number of combatants. The withdrawal fell to the Asian Empire, after two days of clashes.

However, those commanded by Leonidas were betrayed by the Greek Ephialtes of Trachis, who helped the Persian king find an alternative path and surprise his opponents from the rear. With that, it was possible to completely eliminate the small group of Spartan de-

Panoramic view of the Greek island of Paros, region occupied by the troops of Athens during the Persian Wars

fenders. After the clash, the Greek navy received news of the defeat at Thermopylae. After that, the army decided to withdraw to the south, while the Persians expanded their conquests.

The period during which the Persian ruler remained attentive only to the region of Thermopylae allowed the total emptying of Athens, which, subsequently, would be looted and burned by Xerxes' men, as a reprisal for being largely responsible for the outcome of the First Persian Wars. The Athenians proceeded to the island of Salamis, near Athens.

CONSTRUCTION OF THE WOODEN WALL

According to Greek literature, when consulting the oracle of Delphi (dedicated to Apollo, to which the Greeks went to ask questions to the gods), Themistocles heard the following advice: "Protect yourselves with a wooden wall." Despite Athens being already protected by walls, the recommendation was that the Hellenic people should seek naval combat and stay behind the "wooden wall," which represented the naval fleet.

It should be remembered that, since the mid-480s BC, the Athenians started preparing for a war against Persia. In 482 BC, a decision was taken in the city, under the guidance of Themistocles, to build a giant fleet of triremes, essential vessels so that Greece faced

Tomb of the Persian emperor Xerxes I, located in the archaeological site of Naqsh- i Rustam, in Iran, where several monarchs of the ancient empire were buried

the Persians, even with the resistance of members of the Athenian public assembly.

After the Persian victory at Thermopylae and the devastation of Attica in mainland Greece, King Xerxes I entered Athens, also destroying the monuments of the Acropolis, which already housed some of the most famous buildings of the ancient world. The monarch marched on Athens but met no resistance. The sight of the destroyed city offered the Greeks the certainty that there were few chances to maintain freedom in Greece and avoid submission to the Asiatic people.

Meanwhile, Themistocles remained faithful to the plan to attract the Persian fleet and force sea combat. Tradition has it that the general posed as a traitor to the Persian sovereign, inducing him to think that he would win a relatively peaceful victory on the island of Salamis in September 480 BC.

The Spartans and Corinthians defended a military agglomeration on the isthmus (a narrow strip of land that connects a peninsula to a continent), but the Athenian commander concentrated the fleet of about 200 vessels in the bay of Salamis. As planned by Themistocles, the Persian monarch decided to engage in naval combat. Xerxes I authorized the use of a considerable number of ships. The Asian fleet, estimated at 700 ships, lacked coordination when attacking, while the Greeks would occupy the wings, involve the opposing vessels, and push them against each other in order to limit their movements.

According to historical accounts, the strategy resulted in a disagreement among members of the Persian fleet. As a result, the ships collided with each other, and many of them sank. With the arrival of night, the combat came to an end after 12 hours of clashes. The Asian troop withdrew under the eyes of the sovereign Xerxes, who witnessed, from the top of a hill, the Battle of Salamis.

In the evaluation of historians, the Greek resistance against the Persians represented a decisive episode in the history of the European continent. This analysis is based on the fact that, in the event of a Greek capitulation, there would probably be no more barriers for the Persian troops, who would expand the empire across the Old Continent. If the troops of Xerxes I had a positive result, one of the likely scenarios was that Greek culture and the Roman Empire would be supplanted, significantly modifying the history of Western people.

THE PERSECUTION OF THE PERSIANS

After the withdrawal of the Persians from the island of Salamis, General Themistocles intended to take the war to Asia Minor. Therefore, he sent a fleet to the region and promoted the insurrection of the Ionian colonies against the king of Persia. However, the government of Sparta was opposed, for fear of leaving the Peloponnesian Peninsula unprotected.

Thus, the war continued in Europe as the Persian army again invaded Attica in 479 BC. General Mardonius of Persia offered freedom to the Greeks who did not rebel. The atmosphere was so tense that Lycidas, the only member of the Athenian council who voted for submission, was stoned to death by his companions. The conflict made the Athenians seek refuge again in Salamis, as the city was burned a second time.

Upon learning that the Spartan army was marching to help Athens, the Persians withdrew westward to Plataea. The Spartans, known for their excellent military strategies, had another victory over the Persians. According to historians, probably on the same day as the victory in Plataea, the Greek triumph in the naval battle of Mycale, in present-day Turkey, was recorded, which was also a sign for the fight of the Ionians against the Persian administration. Asian troops then withdrew from the region – that was the end of Xerxes I's intentions to conquer Greece. Such episodes marked the end of the Persian Wars; they were fundamental to consolidating

TRIREME, THE GREEK DIFFERENTIAL IN THE WATERS

The trireme was a war vessel used in antiquity by the Greeks and powered by oars. Researchers differ on the origin of the ship, which received this name because the rowers stayed on three decks, which allowed the concentration of more men in a smaller space. The Greek historian Thucydides, for example, reports its use since the 8th century BC.

The use of triremes was essential in Ancient Greece, since the peninsula was surrounded by about 3,000 islands. Vessels formed the majority of Mediterranean navies from 500 BC. The slave- rowing ship boosted classical Greek city-states as naval powers – Athens, in particular –, which, during the wars against Persia, managed 200 ships of this type.

The Greeks built triremes to be fast and highly mobile, making them much easier to maneuver than the galleys of the Persian Empire, which were often used in warfare. The ships covered more than 300 kilometers at a constant speed of 13 km/h.

The standard ship was 36 meters long and had a crew of 150 rowers, whose first line was just 45 centimeters from the waterline. The design was essential in some clashes, for example on the island of Salamis, where the Persians were cornered in a naval battle in 480 BC.

Depiction of the trireme, a fundamental vessel in the victory of the Greeks over the Persians in the Battle of Salamis in 480 BC.

the influence of the Greek people in the Mediterranean Sea.

GREECE FOCUSES ON INTERNAL CONFLICTS

Between 500 BC and 400 BC, Greek territory was the scene of intense and decisive battles, even after the end of one of the main threats: the invasion of the Persian Empire. The atmosphere of tension between the city-states of the region became less intense during the Persian Wars, since they needed, at times, to unite against an external enemy. However, the differences between the governments of each polis surfaced more vigorously after 480 BC, with the resumption of alliances and the attempt to expand influence in the villages.

In general terms, Ancient Greece, in the Classic Period, had Sparta and Athens as the main administrations. Thus, it would be natural for both to dispute space for the realization of political, economic, and territorial conquests. After the Persian Wars, residents of Athens witnessed the golden age of the city, with consolidated democracy and an excellent economy. For this reason, the Athenians increased their power over the region, even starting to collect taxes.

Athens expanded and controlled maritime trade with a powerful naval fleet, enjoying a favorable financial situation, above all, with the formation of the Confederacy of Delos (a military league organized by the city during conflicts against Persian troops). On the other hand, the Spartans already exercised great influence in the Peloponnese Peninsula, mainly after the domination of the city-state of Argos, since 546 BC. In this way, Sparta, commanded by an aristocracy that did not implement Athenian democracy, headed the military alliance called the Peloponnesian League. In case of need, the allies of the two main city-states would be called into battle.

THE CONDITIONS FOR THE PELOPONNESIAN WAR

Relations between Athens and Sparta were tense, although formally friendly, during the Persian Wars, but they got worse from 450 BC on, with frequent struggles over the hegemony dispute in Greece and sporadic truces.

According to the Greek historian Thucydides, Athens' unrivaled power and wealth alarmed the Spartans. The possibility of a war was so considered that Pericles, one of the main Athenian rulers in history, decided to accumulate financial reserves to withstand a large-scale conflict.

The tense situation between the Athenian and Spartan allies led to clashes starting in 431 BC. At the time, the village of Corfu (also called Corcyra, in the western portion of Greece) wanted to sign an alliance with Athens, as the agreement would offer the possibility of dominating trade with the West. However, the place was colonized by the city-state of Corinth, an ally of Sparta in the Peloponnesian League. Thus, Corinth interfered in the negotiations because of the trade dispute, making the situation increasingly favorable to the outbreak of a confrontation.

According to historical records, the trigger for the beginning of the Peloponnesian War was the publication of the Megarian Decree (the name is derived from the city of Megara, an ally of Sparta) by the Athenian Pericles, a kind of trade embargo. According to the published text, traders from Megara (which was located between Corinth and Athens) would be banned from the Athenian market and the colonies. This measure quelled the village's economy and frayed the fragile peace between the Delian and Peloponnesian Leagues. The cities of Megara, Thebes, Sparta, and Corinth allied against Athens and the other members of the Delian League. In 431 BC, forces from Thebes, in central Greece, attacked Plataea, a former ally of Athens, at the beginning of military clashes between the two confederations.

Such confrontations, in general, are divided into three periods. In the first part, between 431 BC and 421 BC, those involved made attempts to destroy the opposing cities but did not achieve satisfactory results. An exception was the episode that directly involved the leaders of the leagues. Sparta and the allies invaded Attica (the region in which Athens is located) in 431 BC. The Athenian administrator Pericles, aware of the superiority of the Spartan land army, convinced his countrymen to take refuge within the walls that connected Athens to the port of Piraeus. The objective was to avoid a battle on land.

The ruler relied on the fleet of triremes to protect the colonies and trade routes, as well as supply the population. However, the

Ancient fortress of Corinth, in the region of the Peloponnese Peninsula.

residents were surprised by the outbreak of an epidemic in 430 BC, known as the "Plague of Egypt" or "Plague of Athens," which killed approximately a third of the population. Not even Pericles resisted the disease.

With this situation, uprisings against the hegemony of Athens in the region started emerging, as, for example, on the island of Lesbos. Although conditions were unfavorable for the Athenians, the naval fleet managed to maintain good performance. Thus, in 423 BC, a one-year truce was established. In 422 BC, the war was evenly matched, and the cities involved were showing signs of wear and tear. The first period of the Peloponnesian War was ended in 421 BC through the Treaty of Nicias (an Athenian military), which would guarantee peace for 50 years. In this context, the allies of Athens sought to free themselves from the imposed conditions that threatened the democratic system, based on the collection of tributes.

THE PELOPONNESIAN WAR: PHASE 2

The truce signed in 421 BC (which was supposed to last five decades) lasted only six years. Thus, the second period of the Peloponnesian War was recorded from 415 BC to 413 BC. The Athenian general and politician Alcibiades led an opposition movement to Sparta in the Peloponnesian Peninsula but did not count on the Spartan victory in the city of Mantineia in 418 BC.

At that time, Athens was already observing the decline of the system that was based on democracy. One way out of the crisis would be a resounding military victory against the Peloponnesian League. In this way, in 415 BC, a powerful fleet was prepared to attack the Sicilian city of Syracuse (in Magna Graecia, in the south of the Italian Peninsula) and nearby regions, in addition to colonies that provided food for Sparta and the allies.

The main defender of the expedition to Sicily, Alcibiades, was accused of ruthlessness by Athenian political opponents. The military then ran away to Sparta and betrayed Athens. The Spartans sent a powerful army to Sicily, which resulted in the Athenian defeat in Syracuse, with serious consequences for the city-state, in 413 BC. In the city of Athens, an oligarchic group in favor of peace took power, establishing a temporary stoppage for the clashes. However, the defenders of the war wanted a quick re-establishment of the conflict.

THE DECLINE OF ATHENS

The third period of the Peloponnesian War started in 412 BC. Generalized uprisings among Athens' allies, in addition to the fortification of Decelia by the Spartans in the region of Attica, put pressure on the city-state, which lost much of its fleet in Sicily. To make things worse, political crises were frequent among residents of Athens. In

Ancient temple in the town of Mantineia, in Arcadia, on the Peloponnese peninsula

parallel, after Alcibiades (who stopped helping Sparta) was appointed "strategos" of the Athenian forces – one of the ten militaries elected annually to take care of defense matters –, the city-state won considerable naval victories between 411 BC and 406 BC.

Concerned about the recovery of Athens, the rulers of Sparta established an alliance with the Persian Empire in exchange for financing a fleet of ships to invade Athens. At the same time, the path would be clear for the Persians to conquer the Greek colonies of Ionia, in Asia Minor.

From then on, the Spartans managed to contain the Athenian advancement, through the tactics of General Lysander. In the following years, Sparta won most of the conflicts that continued the Peloponnesian War. In 404 BC, in the region of Egos- Potamos, the definitive defeat of the Athenians took place. With this setback, Athens was completely surrounded, and the Spartans forced the residents to destroy the fortifications of the place. From then on, Sparta's hegemony would reign over most of the Greek city-states, but for a relatively short period of time.

Shortly after the end of the clashes, there was a turnaround in the policy of Athens, supported by Sparta. The oligarchy took power from the Democrats in an administration known as the "Tyranny of the Thirty," formed by 30 people. The rulers then dissolved the Delian Confederacy and handed over the rest of the Athenian fleet to Sparta. The situation was provisional, as the democratic system returned to force in 403 BC.

The decline of Athens marked the rise of Sparta and undid the only possible way for the unification of the Greek world, hard hit by the return of the cities of Asia Minor to the Persians in exchange for gold. Researchers analyze that the replacement of a project based on trade by a system focused on militarism was the cause of wear and tear in the Hellenic territory. Several villages, previously considered dynamic and full of power, would experience ruin in the economy because of excessive spending on wars and internal disputes. While Greece tried to recover, the Macedonian Empire, to the north of Greek territory, sought to consolidate an expansionist project, emerging as a power in the mid-fourth century BC, under the command of Philip II, who occupied Greece, and his son, Alexander the Great. The conquest put an end to the height period of Athens and Ancient Greece in the Mediterranean Sea.

4

GREECE, THE REFERENCE IN DEMOCRACY

THE EVOLUTION OF THE DEMOCRATIC SYSTEM IN THE CITY-STATE SYMBOL OF VOTING AND DEBATING IDEAS

The influence of the Greek people on Western culture – in particular, the participation of the Athenians – surpassed the geographical borders of the Balkan Peninsula and, mainly, survived the time. The Classic Period (500 BC-338 BC) of Ancient Greece represented a revolution in several areas of human knowledge, such as architecture, engineering, literature, theater, sculpture, and philosophy, among others.

This development left marks that echoed in several people for many centuries. The context at that moment favored the expansion of the ideals of the inhabitants of the Greek territory, especially due to the Athenian protagonism in the political, military, and economic scenario of the time.

The so-called "Golden Age" of Athens was the result of successes in battles, the visionary attitude of a ruler, and the consolidation of a novelty: the democratic system. Therefore, the emergence and evolution of thoughts linked to democracy must be detailed, as well as the other aspects that made the Athenians observe the facts that would be eternalized in the history books, transforming Greece into one of the main references of a nation.

INITIAL CONDITIONS FOR THE DEVELOPMENT OF DEMOCRACY

Historians consider that the initial formation of the democratic system of Athens (the first democracy in the world) occurred around 510 BC. However, the process of constructing democratic ideals dates back to the development of the city-state as a creator of laws.

At the time of the founding of Athens by the Ionian people, political power was under the control of the "Eupatrids," owners of the most productive lands. The command of religion, war and justice was in charge of the "basileus" (sovereigns). Over the years, the basileus lost supremacy and became members of the body that received the name of "Archons," a group of politicians chosen for an annual mandate, and which formed the "Areopagus."

From the 8th century BC onwards, the Athenian political organization underwent several changes, mainly after the territorial expansion that occurred during the Second Diaspora, when the ports and the geographical position of the place favored trade exchange with the colonies. The expansion of economic activities, formerly predominantly linked to agriculture, produced changes in the social status of the city as merchants started pressuring the aristocracy for a greater share of power. In parallel, the poorest portion of the population, without access to any privileges (political or economic), constantly protested against inequalities.

As a result, the owners of fertile lands were forced to make concessions in order to reconcile the conflicts. To this end, they started choosing, among members of the aristocracy, legislators specifically appointed to prepare texts with legal validity. One of the main representatives of the category was Draco, who became a legislator in 621 BC and was responsible for introducing the written record of laws in Athens; until then, they were oral. The city started being ruled based on legislation and no longer according to customs.

NOVELTIES IN THE ATHENIAN LEGISLATION

The Athenian legislator and statesman Solon initiated, in 594 BC, deeper reforms to the code proposed by Draco. He forgave the debts and mortgages of small farmers, which significantly bothered that part of the population, and abolished debt slavery. One of the actions was the creation of "Boule," a council initially formed by 400 members responsible for administrative functions and the preparation of laws. The texts needed to be submitted to the appreciation of the "Ecclesia," or "Assembly," made up of free male individuals. In addition to voting on proposed laws, the group deliberated about matters of general interest.

In the political context, Solon limited the role of aristocrats and increased the number of participants in public life in Athens. The changes proposed by the legislator represented decisive steps towards the development of the democratic environment, consolidated in Cleisthenes' legislation. Despite all the changes promoted by the statesman, tensions continued between the aristocracy, merchants, artisans, and small landowners.

Due to the continuity of the conflicts, a space for a new type of political leader was opened, one that should be capable of articulating the Athenian population against the members of the aristocracy of the city-state. When they came to power, such politicians, called "tyrants," ruled in an authoritarian way and adopted measures aimed at popular appeal. The best known of these was Peisistratus, who remained in power between 560 BC and 527 BC, with intervals.

END OF ATHENIAN TYRANNY

As he belonged to a traditional family of Athens, Cleisthenes obtained the necessary support to overthrow the tyrant Hippias (who ruled the city-state between 527 BC and 510 BC), son of Pisistratus, another tyrant member of a rival family.

According to reports, Hippias would have been about 40 years old when he took power in Athens, continuing the policy of aggrandizing the polis initiated by his father. His younger brother Hipparchus, with whom he would have ruled, was murdered in 514 BC by Athenians known as "Tyrannicides." Thus, the tyrant Hippias, who ruled moderately, integrating aristocrats, started adopting several decisions that went against popular taste. One of the projects stipulated an increase in taxes, necessary to finance the payment of mercenaries hired to defend the ruler from uprisings.

The end of Hippias' career as a tyrant was fulfilled four years later, in 510 BC, when the Spartan king Cleomenes I attacked Athens. Thanks to the help of Athenians opposed to tyranny, Spartan troops surrounded Hippias and his supporters on the Acropolis. The Athens politician decided to abdicate and leave the city. With that, Cleisthenes' family returned from exile, and the politician was

View of the Athenian Agora, the main political space for the development of Greek democracy

able to occupy the government of the city-state.

In the power vacuum in Athens after the expulsion of Hippias, a fundamental clash occurred for the evolution of the democratic ideal. At the time, Cleisthenes sought the support of the population and promised democratic reforms. The promise of these changes would be a response to Isagoras, a political rival, aristocrat, and member of the government who tried to block Cleisthenes' projects. The way out for Isagoras was to call the Spartans to invade Athens once more, but the inhabitants of the polis defended the place. The conflict between the Athenians and the Spartans ended quickly, but it laid the foundations of mistrust between the two city-states, which would result in major battles, such as the Peloponnesian War.

THE GOVERNMENT OF CLEISTHENES

After assuming the Athenian government, Cleisthenes expanded the attributions of the "Ecclesia" and allowed the existence of what the men of the period called "isonomy" (equality before the law) and "isegoria" (equal rights to speak). With that, the politician extended the rights of political participation to all free men born in Athens, called "citizens."

It is worth mentioning, however, that political participation was restricted to 10% of the inhabitants. Foreigners residing in Athens (the so-called "metics"), slaves, and women, among others, were excluded from public life. Projections indicate that, around 500 BC, of the 400,000 residents of the city-state, only 90,000 were considered "citizens." With the reforms of Cleisthenes, the administrative functions were in charge of the "Boule," whose members were raffled among the citizens. The ruler also strengthened the "Ecclesia," which started gathering monthly to discuss the laws.

Military affairs were under the responsibility of the *"strategoi."* Specialists in Ancient Greece also attribute to Cleisthenes the institution of "ostracism," which consisted of the suspension of political rights and the exile of people considered dangerous to the government. In that period, the loss of a citizen's rights was one of the greatest humiliations for the free man of Athens.

In the military aspect, the Athenian citizen lived with the possibility of serving in the army every year. Every 12 months, he could also meet with thousands of colleagues in the "Ecclesia" or be included on the list of 6,000 raffled jurors for the popular courts. At that time, Athenian territory housed thousands of temporary immigrants or immigrants from other Greek cities. It should be remembered that they were not considered citizens either.

Athenian democracy gained strength to consolidate itself in the following century and represent the first system of its type in the history of mankind. Also, according to historians, the emergence of democracy in Ancient Greece was not the result of the planning of a group of thinkers but represented, in fact, a surprise, as it was something unprecedented in the trajectory of human groups.

RELATIONSHIP BETWEEN ECONOMY AND POLITICS

The development of the Athenian democratic system is also directly related to the economic context of the period. A key factor in the opulence seen in Athens between 480 BC (after the end of the Persian Wars, against the Persians) and 404 BC (after the end of the Peloponnesian War, the series of conflicts against Sparta's allies) was the effective use of the silver mines of Laurion, which were 50 kilometers south of the city.

In antiquity, the region was famous for its mineral resources. After the discovery of a gigantic deposit in 483 BC, mining came to represent one of the main sources of income in the municipality, alongside the intense trade. In the same year, the Athenian general Themistocles, already influential and taking advantage of the expanding democratic environment, managed to convince his countrymen to invest the profit from the mines in a fleet of 200 triremes, which would serve to protect the city and would be fundamental to defeating the Persian Empire three years later at the Battle of Salamis.

THE FIRST GREEK COINS

According to historians, the beginning of the 5th century BC witnessed a considerable increase in coin issues in Athens, taking advantage of the growth in silver production in the Laurion mines. In addition, the coin-making process was accelerated in view of preparations to face the Persians in the Second Persian War.

The first coins of Ancient Greece started being minted around the 7th century BC. On the faces, useful objects from everyday life were revealed, in addition to figures of plants and animals, with an emphasis on the owl, the turtle, and the Pegasus (a mythological winged horse representing immortality).

In addition, with a powerful naval fleet, Athens would lead the Delian League, making it important to place the city-state at the highest point of influence over the other Greeks. With mineral resources, Athens paved the way to expand reserves and establish dominance over the waters of the Mediterranean.

The mines were exploited by slaves who belonged to the Athenians, rented by the day. The commercialization of the workforce represented a very precious investment for the municipality. It is worth remembering that the miners had terrible working conditions: they were often trapped in narrow galleries in unhealthy conditions. Because of this, uprisings and escapes were frequent. Slaves took refuge, most of the time, in the temple of Poseidon, located at Cape Sounion, in the south of the Attica Peninsula.

Particularly in relation to Athens, when Peisistratus returned from two exiles and established a more lasting government in the years 540 BC, he introduced a centralized minting, represented by the first issues of figures of owls, which would have lasted throughout the period of tyranny and the beginning of Cleisthenes' democracy.

Progressively, Greek cities started manufacturing coins with divine figures. As an instrument of exchange, coins also came to be considered works of art. Due to the refinement and perfection of the minting, the productions of Ancient Greece acquired unique aspects and spread throughout the Mediterranean Sea.

THE "GOLDEN AGE" OF ATHENS

The facts involved in the evolution of the democratic system were essential for the inhabitants of Athens to verify the splendor of the so-called "Golden Age" under the government of Pericles, a fundamental politician for the development of the city.

It is not known for sure how old the ruler was when he entered political life; it is likely that, at the time, he was over 25 years old. At first, he acted as an assistant to the politician Ephialtes, leader of the democratic wing and mentor to Pericles, known for progressive thinking.

Around 461 BC, the leadership of the democratic party decided to target the Areopagus, a traditional council controlled by the Athenian aristocracy; the state body was once the most important of the polis. Ephialtes then proposed a reduction in the powers of the Areopagus. The Athenian assembly adopted the proposal without much opposition.

Gradually, the democratic party came to be the dominant party in Athenian politics. Pericles, already influential in the city, showed a willingness to follow populist strategies in order to captivate the Athenians. Cimon, from a wealthy family, was the political opponent of the leader of the democratic party and managed to gain popular support. According to researchers, the politician's thinking followed the reasoning that there was no more free space for democratic evolution, contrary to the reflections of Pericles, who, in 461 BC, managed to eliminate his opponent politically through the institution of ostracism. The accusation would be that Cimon would have betrayed the city by acting as a friend of Sparta. The leader of the democratic party became the undisputed sovereign of Athens, who remained in power for nearly four decades until his death, in 429 BC, at the age of 66.

Even after the ostracism of his opponent, Pericles continued to promote a populist social policy. He proposed a decree that would allow the poor to watch theater plays for free, with the state paying the ticket price. In another text, he reduced the property requirements necessary for election to the position of Archon, magistrate of some city-states of Athens in Ancient Greece, in 458 BC, and granted generous salaries to all citizens who served as jurors in the supreme court of Athens. The most controversial measure was a law enacted in 451 BC that restricted Athenian citizenship to anyone whose parents were born there.

Pericles wanted to stabilize Athens' rule over the Delian League, in which the city-state grew into an empire. This occurred because several allies in the confederacy chose to pay tribute to the Athenians instead of providing manpower for the ships in the league's military fleet. Afraid of defeats and fighting in the Aegean Sea region, Athens retained the treasure from Delian alliance (former headquarters of the league and which kept the goods) in 454 BC. It was from the alliance treasure that Pericles extracted the necessary funds to finance the ambitious construction plan in the city, based mainly on the "Acropolis," which included the Propylaea, the Parthenon, and the golden statue of Athena, sculpted by Phidias, a personal friend of Pericles.

In the year 449 BC, Pericles proposed a decree that allowed the use of a large number of resources to finance the main program of reconstruction of the Athenian temples, which made possible the construction of some of the most wonderful artistic creations of the ancient world. At that time, Athens was already experiencing an effervescence in politics, economy, culture, religion, and several other sectors of society.

According to the Roman historian and biographer Plutarch, after assuming the leadership of Athens, Pericles was no longer the same man as before, somewhat submissive to the people. The Greek historian Thucydides, admirer and contemporary of Pericles stated that Athens had a democratic system but was, in fact, "ruled by the first citizen." The biographer even argues that Pericles "led the crowd, rather than being led by it."

THE AGORA IN DETAIL

The agora was surrounded by long *stoai* (plural of *stoa*), wide porticoes that protected visitors from the rain while bringing in light and air. Furthermore, each *stoa* fulfilled an important social function, as it was in these places that citizens met to discuss philosophy, the arts, business, or politics.

The first *stoai* were open at the entrance, with columns flanking the building, and were often done in the Doric style. The buildings were entirely open to the public, where merchants could sell their products. Artists showed their works there, as well as the conducting of religious ceremonies. The *stoai* were usually located around the agoras.

Buildings such as the Royal Stoa and South Stoa I housed those responsible for the daily administration of Athens. Athenian legislators held daily meetings in the so-called "Bouleuterion," located along the west side of the square. The central files were kept in the "Metroon." The forums were located in the northeastern and southern parts of the agora. According to reports, trade activities in this area took place on a daily basis, in the form of large markets, small private shops, and in the streets.

The agora also served as a reference religious center. Therefore, the square had a high number of small shrines and altars; most of them were dedicated to the demigods, known as heroes. As the sacred sites were located at the center of everyday life, they received more regular attention from the population than the large buildings erected on the "Acropolis," the highest region of the city.

The history of the place can be divided into three phases. In the first phase, around 500 BC, the natural slope of the hillside was used. The surface was leveled, and a wall was built on the north side. In the second phase, the orientation of the auditorium was reversed, but the size remained similar. In the third phase, Pnyx was rebuilt and expanded to an audience of approximately 14,000 people. On the occasion, a platform for the speaker, called "Bema," was carved into the rock.

In the 4th century BC, the "Ecclesia" was called at least four times a month to discuss relevant topics indicated by the "Boule." The first meeting of the assembly was called "sovereign," in which vital topics such as grain supply and national defense were discussed. The permanence of officers in the position was also a decision of the body.

The decisions of "Ecclesia" began with the reading of an "agenda," by a representative of the "Boule," with the selected items to be discussed; however, the topics could be changed by the participants. When the matter was presented, the audience was consulted to find out who wanted to deliberate. The most frequent speakers were known as *"hoi politeuomenoi"* (the politicians).

Some officers, such as the "strategoi" (generals), could gain political prominence by demonstrating persuasive power in the assembly with the ability to convince citizens. Pericles, for example, had great influence over the group. After the presentation of opinions by the citizens, a vote was taken by counting the raised hands, characterizing the first direct democracy that is known. Until the beginning of the 5th century BC, the "Ecclesia" accumulated the function of voting laws. However, this function was transferred to the nomothetes (in Greek, "lawmakers"). Finally, the "Boule," in addition to directing the discussions in the assembly, was responsible for verifying compliance with the discussions and for supervising the attitudes of the officers.

THE ATHENIAN ACROPOLIS

The Acropolis of Athens is another symbol of the height of democracy in the city-state. The term originates from the combination, in Greek, of *"akros"* (the highest) and *"polis"* (city). It is a flat-topped rocky hill that rises 150 meters above sea level and houses some of the most famous buildings of the ancient world, such as the Parthenon and the Erechtheion.

It is worth remembering that the acropolis of Ancient Greece originally served as protection against invaders from enemy cities. They were often surrounded by walls. Over time, the sites started serving as civil or religious administrative headquarters. Regarding the beginning of human occupation on the hill, the oldest artifacts date back to the mid-Neolithic period. In the Bronze Age, there were dwellings in the region, as well as workshops, houses and worship space.

Historical records indicate that a temple to Athena Polias (the patroness of the city and other municipalities) was erected around the 6th century BC. At the end of the same century, another temple had been built, the Archaiios Naos ("old temple" in Greek), which may have been dedicated to Athena Parthenos. The building of a new marble temple, the "Old Parthenon," was started at the time of the Battle of Marathon in 490 BC. To accommodate it, the southern portion of the plateau was cleared of obstacles and leveled with the complement of about 8,000 stone blocks from Piraeus, which were up to 11 meters deep, forming a kind of retaining wall.

The Acropolis gate was replaced by the so-called "Ancient Propylaea," an imposing column at the entrance to the hill. The construction remained unfinished for a period due to the Persian invasions in 480 BC. At the time, they were destroyed. Most of the buildings on the Acropolis were erected when the city was under Pericles' command, during the phase known as the "Golden Age," between 460 BC and 430 BC.

Ictinus and Callicrates, two famous architects, and Phidias, one of the main Greek sculptors, were responsible for the rebuilding.

BURIED PERSIAN ART

After the end of the Persian Wars, in 480 BC, the Athenians held purification ceremonies on the Athenian Acropolis, in which they burned and buried the objects of worship and art of the Persian Empire. The celebrations show that most of the temples were preserved in the golden age of the city-state.

Erechtheion, one of the main buildings of the Acropolis of Athens

During the 5ᵗʰ century BC, the acropolis took on its final shape. The statesman Cimon and the general Themistocles ordered the rebuilding of the south and north sides of the walls, while Pericles commissioned the design of the Parthenon. In 437 BC, the architect Mnesicles started elaborating the "Propylaea," with marble columns, partially built on the propylaea of the tyrant Pisistratus; the work was completed in 432 BC.

In the same period, the Athenians started the construction of the Erechtheion, one of the most famous buildings in Athens, which features sculptures in place of columns, for celebrations that included tributes, among others, to the gods and to Erechtheus (the king of the Athenian city-state, according to Greek mythology). Between the Parthenon and the temple of Athena Nice (the Greek goddess who personified victory, strength, and speed, represented by a woman with wings), there was a space destined for the worship of Artemis Bauronia, the goddess represented by a bear. A bronze statue of Athena Promacos (the goddess who fights on the front lines) stands near the Propylaea. The sculpture, standing 9 meters high on a base of almost 2 meters, was also designed by Phidias. In addition, there was the Theater of Dionysus, situated outside the Acropolis. The site was the stage for the greatest plays of antiquity.

THE ATHENIAN DEMOCRACY

According to researchers of procedures linked to Athenian democracy, a series of the decision-making process in the "Ecclesia" could last up to four hours.

POLITICAL TRAJECTORY

In 472 BC, Pericles was responsible for presenting the play "The Persians," by the Greek playwright Aeschylus at the festival of Great Dionysia. The plot deals with a nostalgic vision of the victory of the Athenian forces, commanded by Themistocles, in the Battle of Salamis. According to historians, this situation shows that the young politician supported Themistocles against his political opponent, Cimon, a member of an opposition group that would condemn Themistocles to ostracism.

In the year 463 BC, the statesman was the main prosecutor in charge of prosecuting Cimon, accused of neglecting the vital interests of Athens in Macedonia. Although the defendant was acquitted, the clash exposed the vulnerability of Pericles' main political rival.

Around 461 BC, the leadership of the democratic party decided to propose reforms to the city's deliberative bodies, such as the Areopagus and the Ecclesia. Such changes represented the beginning of a new era, as the group, little by little, became the dominant legend of Athenian politics. Researchers evaluate that Pericles' great influence started being established in that year. In parallel, Pericles showed a willingness to continue with a populist policy, captivating the residents.

As an example, the ruler proposed a decree that would allow the poor to watch theater plays for free, with the state paying the ticket price. In other decisions, Pericles reduced the property requirement necessary for election to the position of Archon (with the power, including, to legislate) in 458 BC, and shortly after, he granted generous salaries to all citizens who served as jurors in Heliaia, the supreme court of Athens. The most controversial measure was a law enacted in 451 BC that limited Athenian citizenship to people whose parents were born in the city-state.

THE ATHENIAN IMPERIALISM

With the sequence of Delian League activities (formed during the Persian Wars), Pericles intended to stabilize Athens' dominance over the alliance and ensure the sovereignty of the city-state in Greek territory. However, it should be noted that the process through which the Delian Confederacy became an Athenian empire is generally considered previous to the period of Pericles' administration. At the time, several allies chose to pay tribute to Athens instead of providing manpower for the ships of the military fleet. The definitive steps in the transition towards the empire may have been triggered by the defeat of Athens in Egypt, which represented a challenge to the city's dominance over the Aegean Sea and led to the uprising of several allies, such as Miletus and Erythras. Historians differ on the decision, but Pericles' administration transferred the alliance treasure from Delos to Athens in 454 BC. Years later, in 449 BC, the uprisings in Miletus and Erythras were quelled. Thus, Athens regained dominance over the allies.

THE RULER OF THE GOLDEN AGE OF ATHENS

The statesman Pericles was born around 495 BC, in the northern region of Athens, and significantly influenced the city-state as a speaker and general. Historians point out that he was one of the main democratic leaders of Athens and the greatest political personality of the 5th century BC. He lived during the Golden Age of Athens and descended, through his mother's lineage, from the Alcmaeonids, an influential and powerful family.

PPericles was the son of the politician Xantippus, who came to command the Athenian contingent in battles. Pericles' mother, named Agariste, played a key role in the beginning of her husband's career. This was because Pericles' mother was the niece of the Athenian reformist Cleisthenes. With that, insertion into political life was a natural path for Pericles.

The concern with education was constant in the life of the young man, who learned music from masters and is considered the first politician to attribute great importance to philosophy – one of the conditions for the prominence of Socrates and Plato in the Athenian scenario of the time. In addition, Pericles enjoyed the company of the philosophers Protagoras, Zeno of Elea, and Anaxagoras.

It was from the alliance treasure that the Athenian ruler extracted the necessary funds to finance the construction plan, which would center on the "Acropolis of Pericles," and included

View of the Athenian Acropolis

the Propylaea, the Parthenon and the golden statue of Athena, sculpted by Phidias, a personal friend of the city-state administrator. In 449 BC, Pericles proposed a decree that allowed the use of considerable sums of money to finance the major rebuilding program of the Athenian temples, which financed some of the wonderful artistic creations of the ancient world.

For more than 20 years, the ruler led several expeditions, most of which took place in the sea. He adopted a cautious tone and based military decisions on the principle adopted by General Themistocles that Athenian predominance depended on naval power. Pericles believed that the Spartans were virtually invincible in land combat. Therefore, the administrator tried to minimize Sparta's advantages by rebuilding the walls of Athens.

In 430 BC, during the Peloponnesian War, the Spartan army looted Attica for the second time. That year, an epidemic devastated the Athenian population. The chaotic condition of the city triggered a wave of revolt among the population, and Pericles was forced to defend himself in an emotional final speech. The text is considered a prayer of exceptional content, which reveals Pericles' virtues in oratory, but also his bitterness due to the ingratitude of his compatriots.

Initially, the argumentation was successful, and the administrator managed to get through the crisis. However, Pericles' political enemies achieved the objective shortly after, with Pericles being removed from the position of general in addition to receiving a fine.

Athenian politics, full of twists and turns, produced one more of them in little less than a year: in 429 BC, the Athenians forgave the commander and reelected him to the military command of the city-state. He then led all operations that year, once again taking control of power in the city. In the same year, however, Pericles would suffer a hard blow due to the deaths of his two sons, Paralus and Xantippus, victims of the epidemic. Debilitated, the general also contracted the disease in the autumn of 429 BC; he did not resist and died.

POLITICAL TENSION IN ATHENS

Difficulties in politics weighed heavily on Pericles' last days. It is worth remembering, for example, that far more people died in the plague than would have died in war. The Athenians held him responsible for the war with the Spartans and for misguided strategy in battles.

With the death of Pericles, Athens was deprived of an administrator with extraordinary qualities, as he was a military man and strategist of great importance, as well as a politician with unusual talent. He was capable of formulating a policy and convincing the Athenians to faithfully adopt it, based on democratic precepts. In addition, Pericles prevented citizens from acting hastily and encouraged them in moments of low confidence. After being re-established in power, the leader was capable of uniting the Athenians around several ideas, as perhaps no other Athenian could.

Pericles, in a famous speech delivered at the end of the first year of the Peloponnesian War

5

THE SCHOOL OF SOCRATES

HOW THE LOVE FOR REFLECTION AND THE
SEARCH FOR TRUTH LED THE GREEKS TO FOREVER
INFLUENCE THE WESTERN WORLD

With the consolidation of the democratic system and the government of Pericles, the Athenians experienced heights in the economic aspect and in other areas of daily life, such as the arts, architecture, and literature. One of the main fields that registered significant evolution was philosophy, mainly due to the reflections provided by Socrates and his disciples.

In that period, around 430 BC, the foundations that guide, until today, the philosophical thought of the West were laid. However, it is attributed to Thales of Miletus, who lived between 624 BC and 556 BC, the first records linked to philosophy in Ancient Greece.

THE STAGES OF PHILOSOPHICAL THINKING IN GREECE

In general terms, Greek philosophy can be divided into three major periods, known as the pre-Socratic, Socratic, and Hellenistic periods.

The pre-Socratic philosophers developed theories from the 7th century BC to the 5th century BC. They received this denomination because they preceded Socrates, the greatest exponent in the field until today. Men sought in the elements of nature the answers about the origin of being and the world. Therefore, they were called "philosophers of physis."

The basis for the development of philosophy refers to literature. Greek poets, like Homer, played an important role in educating young people. The Homeric poems presented characteristics that would serve as a basis for the evolution of the area. The main one is the search for the causes of the narrated events, seeking a language that dealt with reality in the most complete way possible.

Hesiod, another Greek poet, had a great importance to Greek thinking for having narrated the birth of the gods, a way of trying to explain the origin of the universe, a theme that would appear in the works of Thales of Miletus.

DID YOU KNOW?

Aristotle (384 BC to 322 BC) was the first to state that whales and dolphins are not fish and that bats are not among birds. The philosopher recorded approximately 500 different classes of animals and dissected about 50 of them.

Miletus Ruins, in Asia Minor, in present-day Turkey, hometown of Thales, considered the first Greek philosopher

THE BASES OF WESTERN PHILOSOPHY

The Socratic period, also called the Classic period, marks the impulse for philosophical aspects to be discussed more comprehensively, the focus of analysis being replaced. In this phase, philosophers started being concerned with problems related to the individual and the organization of humanity.

They started questioning themselves about good, truth, and justice, among many other aspects. Thus, nature ceased to be the main object of philosophical investigation, which focused on the human being. For this reason, the figure of Socrates emerges as the greatest representative of this transition, which has influenced Western thinking until the present time.

Marble sculpture in honor of the Greek poet Hesiod, whose records helped the emergence of the so-called philosophy of Ancient Greece

THE LEGACY OF SOCRATES

In the work "Phaedo," the death of Socrates was narrated like this by Plato: "He raised the cup to his lips and very naturally, without hesitating a bit, drank until the last drop. Until that moment, most of us had managed to hold back tears; however, when we saw him drinking and that he had drunk everything, no one could stand it anymore. I could not help myself either. I cried with a living tear. Covering my head, I mourned my misfortune; yes, it was not because of misfortune that I was crying, but because of my own luck, seeing what kind of friend I would be deprived of. Crito stood up before me, unable to hold back his tears. Apollodorus, who had not stopped crying from the beginning, started roaring, his weeping and lamentations moving all those present to their hearts, with the exception of Socrates himself."

Socrates caused an unprecedented break in the history of Greek philosophy. While the pre-Socratic philosophers, called naturalists, sought to answer questions related to nature, the thinker contributed by encouraging people to participate in the discovery of evidence, the manifestation of the inner master to the soul. To know oneself, then, would be to know God in oneself.

Socrates' method gained prominence, as it was based on argu-

Ruins of the city of Magnesia, in Greek territory, where meteoric rocks were found and researched by Thales of Miletus

mentation. He insisted that truth can only be discovered through the use of reason. The legacy resided, above all, in the unshakable conviction that even the most abstract questions admit a rational analysis, which was until today one of the main keys of Western thinking.

Philosopher Thales of Miletus was the first to understand and spread the dynamics of the eclipse of the Sun

THALES, THE "FATHER" OF GREEK PHILOSOPHY

Thales of Miletus was an ancient Greek philosopher, mathematician, engineer, and astronomer. He was born in Miletus, a former Greek colony, in Asia Minor (now Turkey), around 624 BC. Records indicate that the philosopher died in approximately 546 BC.

He is appointed as one of the main sages of the Greek territory. The mathematician considered water to be the origin of everything. The followers agreed with the engineer regarding the existence of a "single principle" for the primordial nature of matter, although they disagreed regarding the "primordial substance," which constituted the essence of the universe. Thus, the observation of nature and the relationship between resources and human beings represented one of the basic tasks of those who ventured in the early days of philosophy.

Thales was the first to explain the solar eclipse, by noting that the moon is illuminated by the star. According to the Greek historian Herodotus, the mathematician would have predicted a solar eclipse in 585 BC, a feat that, according to the philosopher Aristotle, marks the moment when, in fact, philosophy begins.

In general, the mathematician made an effort to seek the single principle of explanation for the world. With this, Thales constituted the ideal of this area of research and provided a boost for its own development.

The philosopher's tendency to seek the truth of life in nature also led him to experiments with magnetism, which, at that time, existed only as a curiosity, such as the attraction of iron objects for a type of meteoric rock found in the city of Magnesia, from which the name derives.

PHILOSOPHICAL SCHOOLS OF THE HELLENISTIC PERIOD

The term "Hellenistic" derives from Hellenism, which corresponds to the period of Macedonian rule, under the command of Alexander the Great, until the Roman occupation of Greek territory. Generally speaking, this is the period that goes from the end of the 4th century BC to the end of the 1st century AD. It is in this phase of Western thinking that philosophy expands from Greece to other knowledge centers, such as Rome and Alexandria.

The Hellenistic schools have characteristics similar to those of the Socratic (or classic) period, such as the search for wisdom, defined by philosophers as the most recommended therapy to care for tranquility in everyday aspects of life. Such institutions carried Socrates' legacy by admitting that men remain ignorant and are harmed by the value judgments attributed to things. For this reason, according to thinkers, citizens should change the way they reason. For them, this would only be possible with inner peace.

Among the currents of thinking of the Hellenistic period, the dogmatists stand out, for whom the challenge consists of transforming value judgments. Skeptics and cynics believe that the goal is to interrupt all judgments.

Illustration depicting the philosopher Socrates

SEX FOR REPRODUCTION

A current of researchers believes that Socrates was homosexual and defended this type of relationship as the highest inspiration for those considered "right- thinking men." According to interpretations, for the philosopher, sex between a man and a woman would only serve as a means for reproduction. The love between two men was considered, by the culture of some Greek city-states, to be the only true love.

DID YOU KNOW?

During his childhood, Socrates helped his father with his craft. However, according to reports, he had difficulties working marble. Socrates was married to Xanthippe, who was much younger than him and had a son, Lamprocles. There are reports that the couple may have had two more children, Sophroniscus and Menexenus.

SOCRATES: THE MOST INFLUENTIAL PHILOSOPHER OF ANCIENT GREECE

Details about the life of Socrates come from the dialogues of Plato (a pupil of the philosopher), the plays of Aristophanes, and the dialogues of Xenophon. There is no evidence that Socrates, on his own initiative, has published works.

The thinker was born on the plains of Mount Lycabettus, near Athens, in 469 BC. Socrates came from a family with humble origins. He was the son of Phaenarete, a midwife, and Sophroniscus, a sculptor who specialized in carving columns in temples.

Interestingly, Socrates used to walk barefoot and was not in the habit of bathing. On certain occasions, he stopped what he was doing and meditated on a problem, remaining still for hours. The thinker was in the habit of debating with the inhabitants of Athens. Unlike the pre- Socratics, the philosopher did not find a school and preferred to carry out his work in public places, especially in squares and gymnasiums. Still, according to reports, he acted in a relaxed and uncompromising way, something unusual at that time.

It is not known for sure what Socrates' daily occupations were. According to some sources, the thinker learned the profession of a potter from his father. In Xenophon's work, Socrates appears to declare that he was dedicated to the maieutic (the birth of ideas), considered by him the most important occupation.

For Socrates, before seeking any truth, man needs to analyze himself and recognize his own ignorance. Socrates starts a discussion and leads his interlocutor to such recognition through dialogue, which represents the first phase of his method, called "irony" or "refutation." In the second phase, Socrates asked for several particular examples of what was discussed. For example, if he was looking to define prudence, he asked for descriptions of acts considered prudent. Soon after, the thinker analyzed the cases in order to discover what was similar in all of them. This common thing is prudence, the essence of wise acts, which will exist in any prudent act.

RELATIONSHIP WITH POLITICS

Socrates despised politics and did not adapt to public life, although he had exerted functions in the political framework, including as a soldier. His ideal philosophical method was dialogue, through which he communicated as best he could with his contemporaries, in an effort to transmit knowledge to Greek citizens. In addition to leaving the world his unparalleled wisdom, he also educated Plato and Xenophon, fundamental disciples for the perpetuation of his teachings, although he did not leave the result of his preaching in writings. According to reports, Socrates married Xanthippe but never prioritized family. He believed that the critical essence led him to a mission, that of multiplying beings equally endowed with wisdom. The choice would lead him to clash with the rulers' summit, in which he would conquer enemies and dissatisfaction. The critical character and thoughts opposed to the social structure upset the protagonists of the Greek political scene.

In this way, Socrates' ideas spread throughout the city, while he gained disciples. With the outbreak of the Peloponnesian War, all men between the ages of 15 and 45 were sent to fight. Socrates, for his ability to make people follow him, was chosen as one of the generals. At the end of the clashes, with the intention of saving the few living soldiers, the thinker ordered everyone to return quickly to Athens but leave the dead on the battlefield, contrary to a law that obliged the general to bury all dead soldiers or die trying. So, upon arrival, he was arrested.

The thinker's behavior resulted in his arrest, accused by the Athenians of perverting youth and denying the worshiped gods. Before the court, he refused to defend himself, as he did not intend to renounce what he believed and what he preached to his countrymen. He preferred to be condemned and preserve the search for the truth. With this decision, he chose death, decreed by the judges through a majority vote.

The court, made up of 501 citizens, condemned the thinker. But the sentence was not the death penalty. The jurors knew that if they condemned Socrates to death, thousands of young people would revolt. They condemned the philosopher to exile forever or to have his tongue cut out. With that, he could not teach others. If he refused to serve the sentence, he would be killed.

The prison that housed Socrates, in Athens, before the death sentence handed down by Greek justice

AFTER THE CONDEMNATION, THE PHILOSOPHER STATED:

"You leave me the choice between two things: one, which I know is horrible, which is living without being able to pass on my knowledge. The other, which I do not know, is death... I therefore choose the unknown!"

When addressing the Athenian citizens who were judging him, Socrates said that he was grateful to them and that he loved them, but that he would obey the gods rather than them. According to the thinker, as long as he had a breath of life, the jury could be sure that he would not stop philosophizing, his only concern was walking the streets. The objective was to convince his countrymen not to worry about the body or wealth, but mainly about the soul, in order to make it as good as possible.

After that, Socrates left the court and went to prison. At that time, there was a law that required that no executions take place during the voyage of a sacred ship to Delos. In this way, Socrates was imprisoned for 30 days in Athens, under the custody of 11 magistrates in charge of penitentiary administration. For a month, the thinker received his friends and talked to them. He declared that he did not want to break the laws of the country and refused the help of his companions to escape. In 399 BC, Socrates drank hemlock (a poisonous plant from the Northern Hemisphere) and, in front of his friends, died of poisoning.

DID YOU KNOW?

Socrates was one of the few Greek philosophers not to write any works, as he had contempt for writing. The thinker preferred dialogue as a way to reach the truth. The books that are credited to Socrates were, in fact, composed by his disciples.

6

GREEK MYTHOLOGY: GODS AND HEROES

THE LEGENDS ASSOCIATED WITH THE CULTURE
OF ANCIENT GREECE DATE BACK TO 700 BC
AND TELL STORIES OF CHARACTERS WHO STILL
INFLUENCE LITERARY WORKS TODAY

The richness of Greek culture is presented in different ways. Within this reality, mythology is one of the most important flags and has, over time, influenced literary and artistic creations around the world. In Brazil, one of the clearest examples is the work of Monteiro Lobato, who appropriated such legends to compose many of his stories in the late 1930s and early 1940s.

In summary, Greek mythology can be defined as a set of myths about different gods, centaurs, heroes, titans, and nymphs. Such fables originated at the junction of Doric and Mycenaean mythologies, approximately in 700 BC.

The Mycenaeans, who lived between the years 1,600 BC and 1,050 BC and developed on the island of Crete, had different beliefs from the older Greek civilizations, which were worshipers of a mother goddess. They praised Poseidon, as they believed him to be the ultimate ruler of the Earth. Most historians understand that, at that time, the proliferation of the first legends of Greek mythology began, since, in that period, the main god of that people became Zeus.

In mythology, the Greek gods were characterized by having human forms and feelings, such as love, anger, and envy. These simi-

Homer describes in "Iliad" and "Odyssey" the deeds of characters from Greek mythology

larities between gods and men are one aspect of Greek humanism. By being subject to such inclinations, they commonly fell in love with earthly beings and reproduced with them. Certain well-known heroes were considered children of gods; however, they continued to be human and finite. On the other hand, the gods had the gift of immortality.

WRITINGS

Within this polytheistic context – the worship of several gods – the existence of any sacred scripture is not observed in Greek mythology, as the Bible is for Christians or the Koran for Muslims. Writings about the subject were drawn up by Hesiod ("Theogony") and Homer ("Iliad" and "Odyssey") during the 7ᵗʰ century BC.

Also known as "Genealogy of the Gods," "Theogony" is a mythological poem in 1,022 hexameter verses written and narrated by Hesiod which deals with the emergence and history of the Greek gods.

Homer, on the other hand, describes in his books, considered the most important in history, the great deeds of mythological characters.

MYTHOLOGY AS AN IDEOLOGICAL INSTRUMENT

Hesiod's "Theogony" is a collection of stories that speak of the hierarchy and genealogy of heroes and gods. Despite the view that Greek mythology was drawn up to explain the origins of the universe and men, several historians today understand that it also worked as a kind of ideological instrument used to maintain aristocratic rule in pre-democratic Greece.

"Theogony" is a book supported by three pillars. First, the "Cosmogony" ("cosmos" = universe; "gony" = origin) provides a very comprehensive report of the beginning of the world. At this moment, the author addresses four gods: Chaos (the chaotic nothing that later takes shape and is the origin of everything); Gaia (Mother Earth); Tartarus (the subterranean world, later called "hell" by the Christian world); and Eros (love and desire). The four gods represent the image that starts with the pre-genesis (formless matter) and goes through the verification of its formation with Gaia and, then, the phenomenon of the emergence and disappearance of beings.

Through Chaos, Erebus and Nyx (the night) sprang up. From this second were born Ether and Hemera (the day). From the union between Tartarus and Gaia emerged Uranus (the sky), Oureas (the mountains), and Pontus (the sea). Thus ends the first stage of "Cosmogony."

The second part of the work, in turn, deals with the sovereignty of Uranus. He united with Gaia, his mother. Together, they generated the Titans (Hyperion, Iapetus, Cronus, Oceanus, Coeus, and Crius), the Cyclopes, the Hecatonchires, and the Titanides (Tethys, Phoebe, Mnemosyne, Theia, and Rheia). In addition to this union, other relationships give rise to different gods and demigods. The objective of this part of the book was, properly speaking, to report the so-called "Theogony" ("theos" = gods; "gony" = origin).

It is said that Cronus, the god of time, was one of the children of Uranus and would have castrated his own father. Thus, he would take power. From sperm spilled into the ocean, a foam emerges and gives rise to Aphrodite. Cronus marries his sister, Rhea, and gives rise to the second generation of deities (Hestia, Demeter, Hera, Hades, Poseidon, and Zeus).

The future scenario shows an environment in which order and peace are replaced by passing domains. Cronus, when begetting, swallowed his children. However, by chance, Zeus, the youngest, is hidden. The father swallows a stone in his place, believing it to be his youngest son. With that, Zeus managed to grow up, dethroning Cronus and making him vomit all his siblings, who proclaimed him the new god-king. Zeus, then, reached power after arduous battles and originated a new phase.

Finally, the work presents the "Heroogony." This stage shows Zeus established as the dominator and his consequent adventures. The god-king forms, through his constant sexual union with mortals and goddesses, a new generation of hero demigods, like his son Heracles (Hercules for the Latins).

Faced with the history of dethronement of their predecessors, the gods started creating certain barriers for their successors so that no more episodes of dethronement would happen.

The genealogies and also the stories of these gods, demigods, and heroes helped to understand the phases of man, traditionally called Gold, Silver, and Bronze. According to historians, the purpose of this analogy was to clearly demonstrate the degeneration of man from a superior race to an inferior one. That is, just as there was a hierarchy among the gods, the same would need to happen among men, who should obey such laws, as this was the destiny of the cosmos. This idea was more easily disseminated because the ancient Greek man saw himself as an integral part of the cosmos and ended up consenting to this favorable speech about the order of things. Names related to deities were placed on founded cities. Kings, on the other hand, sought to justify their position of power based on their supposed descent from mythological gods.

Within the hierarchical scale of Greek mythology, the Olympian gods are considered the most powerful among several existing groups. The Greek people believed that the deities inhabited the top of Mount Olympus, the highest mountain in the country, from where they decided about the lives of mortals. A group of twelve members form the upper class of Greek gods.

ZEUS, THE RULER OF ALL GODS

Among the gods of the upper class, Zeus is considered the ruler of the others. The god of thunder and lord of Olympus was, as previously described, the youngest son of Cronus and Rhea. He survived his father's habit of devouring his children, and took power from his parent.

It is said that Zeus was raised in the woods of Crete and had honey and goat's milk as his main food items. As an adult, he looked for his father to confront him, and the two became enemies. It was then that the Lord of Olympus forced Cronus to drink a magic potion that brought back the children he had swallowed in the past. In this way, Zeus met four siblings: Demeter, Poseidon, Hestia, and Hades.

After ten years of battle, Zeus destroyed Cronus and took Olympus alongside the brothers Poseidon and Hades, who helped him in the war against their father. From there, they started commanding everything on Earth and in Heaven. All were under their rule.

Zeus had powers related to atmospheric phenomena. He produced lightning and thunder. With his right hand, he sent rain. He was married three times, the last time to Hera, and had many heirs. It is worth mentioning that Hera demonstrated jealous and aggressive behavior, since Zeus had several lovers and several children out of wedlock. It was believed that Zeus was the god who gave man the path of reason. He also taught that true knowledge is achieved only through pain.

The jealous Hera, wife of Zeus, was considered the protector of marriages

HERA, THE PROTECTOR OF MARRIAGES

Queen of Olympus, Hera ruled alongside her husband Zeus. However, she, who considered marriage to be very important, was humiliated by her unfaithful husband. Mythology tells us that she became even more depressed when, alone, Zeus begat his daughter Athena. With this, he indicated that he did not need his wife, not even to conceive.

In one of the episodes of jealousy, Hera meets the goddess Callisto, who had conquered her husband through beauty and transformed her into a bear. In the face of this, Callisto was isolated and frightened in the forest because of the hunters. One day, she recognized her son, Arcas, and ran to hug him. However, because he did not distinguish the mother, he prepared his spear against Callisto. Seeing what would happen, Hera cast a spell and sent both to the heavens, where they became constellations: Ursa Major (Great Bear) and Ursa Minor (Lesser Bear). Considered the protector of married women, the goddess Hera pursued, for a long time, not only the lovers but also all the children that her husband Zeus had out of wedlock.

APOLLO, THE GOD OF LIGHT

The god Apollo is also known as Phoebus (bright). Within Greek mythology, he is considered the god of light and youth. Apollo, son of Zeus and the Titan Leto, had Artemis as his twin sister. According to legend, he and his sister were born on the island of Delos, where their mother Leto sought refuge from Hera, wife of Zeus.

Apollo was recognized as an excellent archer. It is said that, with only a year of life, he followed the snake Python, his mother's enemy, and killed it with arrows. His bow fired lethal darts, which killed men suddenly.

Within the context of Greek mythology, Apollo is seen as a fair and pure god, as he helped patients cure different diseases through sleep.

ATHENA, THE GODDESS OF WISDOM

Named Minerva by the Romans, Athena was the Greek goddess of arts and wisdom. She was conceived through the union of Zeus and the goddess Metis. Athena was a beautiful virgin goddess and a warrior.

Mythology highlights that she was the favorite daughter of Zeus. However, when her mother, Metis, got pregnant, Zeus swallowed his wife in fear that his daughter would be born with more powers than himself and could take away his throne. After a few years, Zeus, with a very strong headache, asked Hephaestus to hit him with an ax. In this way, Athena, already an adult, jumped out of her father's brain. Once, Athena and her uncle, Poseidon, disputed the post of patron/patroness of an important Greek city. She won a contest, and the town was named after Athens. Athena was recognized as the goddess of reflection, prudence, and mental power, as well as a lover of beauty and perfection.

APHRODITE, THE GODDESS OF LOVE

One of the most famous characters in Greek mythology, Aphrodite is the goddess of love, beauty, and sex. She corresponds to Venus in Roman mythology. She was extremely revered in cities like Sparta, Athens, and Corinth.

Historically, there are two versions of her birth, which would have taken place on the island of Cyprus. For Hesiod, Aphrodite was born in a quite unusual way. The author states that, after Cro-

The painting "The Birth of Venus" (Sandro Botticelli, 1484) depicts Aphrodite, the goddess of love

nus cut the organs of Uranus (his father) and threw them into the sea, a white foam was formed around these, which mixed with salt water and originated Aphrodite. On the other hand, Homer simply explains that the goddess of love was the daughter of Zeus and Dione (the goddess of nymphs).

Married to Hephaestus, the god of fire, she was not faithful to her husband. On the contrary, she had countless lovers. These were extramarital affairs with mortal men and other gods. From these romances, several children were generated.

Even though she was known as the goddess of love, Aphrodite had many enemies, such as Hera and Athena.

The festivities that honored Aphrodite had as priestesses the so-called sacred prostitutes. Sexual relations with them were considered a ritual of worship. Aphrodite was portrayed in the Renaissance period by several painters, such as Sandro Botticelli, author of the work "The Birth of Venus."

ARES, THE GOD OF WAR

Ares, son of Zeus and Hera, is known as the Greek god of war. He was famous for his bloodlust. He had inherited his father's strength and his mother's bad temper. Furthermore, he, who ruled the city of Sparta, greatly appreciated battles and fights. The god of war had a forbidden love affair with Aphrodite. Among the children he had with the wife of Hephaestus, two accompanied him in wars: Deimos and Phobos.

However, Aphrodite's husband discovered the betrayal and decided to prepare an ambush for both of them. He placed an invisible net on the bed, trapped them, and the act was witnessed by all the other gods. After being released, they separated. Ares, as a Roman god, fathered the twins Remus and Romulus with Rhea.

In battles, her main enemy was the goddess Athena, a strategist. Ares had a very different profile and preferred bloodier fights. He was defeated by Athena on several occasions.

During the wars, he used a spear, shield, helmet, and breastplate. He also had a wagon driven by four horse-like animals that breathed fire through their nostrils.

ARTEMIS, THE GODDESS OF HUNTING

Artemis, the twin sister of Apollo, was the deity responsible for hunting. He represented sunlight, while she symbolized the moon. Her mother was pursued by Hera. Leto, expecting her two children, arrived as a refugee on the island of Delos and gave birth on Mount Cinto. First came Artemis, who received bows and silver arrows as a gift from her father. In the sequence, Apollo won the same items, but made of gold.

Greek mythology tells us that, as a child, she asked her father to fulfill her biggest wish in celebration of her birthday. Artemis requested to have the power to walk freely in the woods, amidst wild animals. The other request was to be free from the obligation to marry. Her two wishes came true. The goddess of hunting was particularly worshiped by the nymphs, and danced with them in the forests under the moonlight.

POSEIDON, THE GOD OF THE SEA

Poseidon, the god of the sea, was strong and sported a voluminous beard. He inhabited the sea depths. With his famous trident, he made water sprout from the ground and generated huge tidal waves. Among the Romans, he was known as Neptune.

He was the husband of Amphitrite. With her, he had a son named Triton. In addition to his wife, the god of the sea had many other lovers during his lifetime. With these out-of-wedlock lovers, he fathered other children, some known for their cruelty. The most notorious were Cyclops and the giant Orion. Poseidon is also the father of Pegasus, the winged horse sired by Medusa.

It is also said that, in the Trojan War, Poseidon helped the king in the construction of the city walls. For the help, a reward was promised, which was never fulfilled. With a lot of anger, he took revenge on Troy by sending a creature from the sea to loot that land. The god of the sea was celebrated through mystical games and competitions that took place every two years.

HEPHESTUS, THE GOD OF FIRE AND METAL

Hephaestus, the god of fire, was also famously known as the protector of metal-related activities. He was born with a quite ugly appearance and with dwarfism. Because of this, Hera, his mother, would have thrown Hephaestus into the waters of the sea. However, the goddess Thetis, in a gesture of generosity, took him in.

After being cared for by Thetis for nine years, he developed an ability to work with metals and jewels. The god of fire produced the thunder and lightning of Zeus through the powers he carried with him. Hephaestus also drew up the Trident of Poseidon and the arrows of Apollo, in addition to the armor of Achilles in the Trojan War.

DEMETER, THE GODDESS OF AGRICULTURE

In Greek mythology, Demeter was the one who guaranteed nutrients for the land and the consequent success of the country's agriculture. In addition, she had the function of protecting marriages and pregnancies.

The story tells that she had her daughter Persephone kidnapped by Hades, who lived in hell. There, the two were married. Despite this, Demeter managed to have her daughter spend part of the time with her and part of the time with her husband in the depths of Hell.

According to the writings, when Persephone was with her

mother, spring prevailed on Earth. In turn, when she returned to her husband's room, winter appeared.

The goddess of agriculture traveled numerous times alongside Dionysus to teach and help men care for the land and crops.

HESTIA, THE GODDESS OF THE SACRED FLAME

The daughter of Cronus and Rhea was considered the virgin goddess of the family. Hestia represented the flame that remained lit in Greek homes. This fire, according to mythology, was a symbol of light and peace. In this way, the flame of the goddess would have to be permanently lit both in houses and in temples.

One of her main functions was to indicate the importance of the family in social life in Ancient Greece. It was rarely present in works of art. When depicted in paintings, she appeared in a white dress with a veil covering her face. The white clothes showed her purity.

Whenever a Greek city was inaugurated, the people of that locality lit a fire in the place where the political center would be. It was the way they found to reach the protection of the goddess.

Demeter, the goddess of agriculture, depicted on a marble statue in Ukraine

HERMES, THE MESSENGER OF THE GODS

Also called the god of travelers and divination, Hermes was considered the patron of thieves and cheaters. In addition to being a messenger of the gods, the son of Zeus and the nymph Maia was a faithful emissary from the world of darkness.

According to mythology, Hermes, as a child, jumped out of his cradle and stole the flock of his brother Apollo. To mislead him, he put his sandals on backward so that his brother would go the wrong way. Afraid of being tricked again, Apollo ordered Hermes to swear that he would never trick him again. In return, he promised to make him rich, honorable, and skilled in whatever he did honestly. Thus, with the promise fulfilled, Hermes became the master of the four elements.

For a long time, he was worshiped in Greece as the god of fertility, flocks, magic, and travel. He also became a patron of the souls of the dead who went to Hell.

MYTHOLOGY AND ITS HEROES

Despite the sovereign presence of its countless gods, Greek mythology is also highlighted by its heroes. Some are children of the gods themselves with humans. The most important names are Achilles, Odysseus, and Heracles (Hercules, for the Romans).

As narrated in the book Iliad, Achilles was a character of the Trojan War. The story tells that he was dipped in the Stype River by Thetis, his mother, so that he became immortal. To this end, Thetis held him by his heels, which remained the only vulnerable part of him.

THE LOWER CLASS OF GREEK GODS

In addition to the 12 gods of the upper class, Greek mythology also mentions three deities that were considered lower: Hades, Dionysus, and Pan.

Hades, brother of Zeus, is known as the god of Hell. He had dominion over the realm of the dead, a place filled with sadness and pain. He reached this rank battling against the Titans and won alongside Poseidon and Zeus.

Dionysus (Bacchus, for the Romans) was the god of wine and pleasure. To him was transmitted the art of growing grapes.

Another lower deity is Pan, the god of forests. He was considered a protector of groves and shepherds. He would have been born with the horns and legs of a goat.

Nymphs, in turn, were widely known as the great guardians of nature. They also represented the arts and sciences.

*This statue of Achilles adorns the gardens
of the Achilleion Palace, Greece*

7

WAY OUT TO THE SEA

ANCIENT GREECE OVERCAME THE
DIFFICULTIES IMPOSED BY ITS
MOUNTAINOUS RELIEF AND INVESTED IN
MARITIME INCURSIONS TO EXTRAPOLATE
BORDERS AND EXPAND ITS TRADE

An economy that moved according to the geographic characteristics of the country. That was Ancient Greece. The mountainous relief became a challenge to overcome in carrying out trade transactions at the time. The difficult situation led to the emergence of small and sparse communities in that region.

However, the difficulties did not cool the economy. Quite the opposite. The Greeks looked for a viable alternative, and the sea was the solution they found. Maritime transactions became important allies in the economy of Ancient Greece.

The main export products of the metropolis were ceramics, wine, and olive oil. On the other hand, its colonies worked in the supply of items such as metals, wood, cereals, furs, and wool. In general, agriculture and crafts were the most important and notorious activities of the city-states. Despite the natural barriers, the economy of Ancient Greece could be considered quite dynamic. So much so that it is highlighted as one of the ancient civilizations with the greatest economic development.

AGRICULTURE AND LIVESTOCK

It may sound strange that agriculture is so important in a nation with such mountainous land. However, history shows that the activity was largely carried out in the so-called fertile valleys. Over time, vast plantations – used as a livelihood – formed the basis of the Greek economy.

Among the most cultivated products were olives, grapes, and cereals. The grapes had as their main destination the production of wines, and the olives were transformed into liters and more liters of olive oil. They harvested the barley and wheat in the spring. Autumn was the time for the harvest to be done among the olive trees and the vines.

Vegetables, herbs, and fruits – especially apples, figs, and pomegranates – were also part of ancient Greek agricultural culture. However, the internal population growth, mainly from the 5th century BC, made it necessary to import innumerable agricultural products.

CRAFT

In addition to its evident artistic importance, the craft was configured as an economic activity of huge relevance in Ancient Greece. Artificers were responsible for most of the products drawn up in the country. Free men and servants often worked side by side, receiving the same wages. In general, artisans made the most varied goods. These were weapons, several tools, furniture, ceramic objects (tiles, plates, and pots) jewels, shoes, and wool fabrics, among others.

Decorated amphorae became one of the main elements of local craft. They were used, above all, to transport liquids, such as perfumes, wine, and olive oil. At the time, Greek ceramics were considered the best in the entire ancient world. Miletus, Corinth, and Rhodes were great centers of ceramic. On the other hand, Athens and Megara were among the most important cities producing fabrics. The people of Thasos gained fame on account of their gold, and the people of Athens for their silver. Corinth made bronze items, and Chalcis made copper items. Several cities had shipyards. Most localities had small factories that produced breastplates, furniture, and kitchen utensils.

Other locations ended up becoming famous for producing very specific items. Cyrene, for example, grew silphium, a medicinal plant. Cythera was extremely well known for its purple dye. Tanagra was a producer of clay figurines in the shape of people and animals. The best quality olive oils were found in Lesbos and Athens.

Agricultural activity took place in the plains of Laconia and Messenia, in the south of the country. However, elsewhere in Greece, farmers cultivated their land themselves. They formed terraces on the small properties that lay on the slopes of the hills. The Greeks carried out manual farming work. They used precarious plows with animal traction – usually oxen – and mattocks. They cultivated only part of the fields during the year. The other part remained resting so that the land remained fertile. They, however, never irrigated the soil and made little use of the advent of fertilizers.

On the other hand, livestock did not have the same development success among the Greeks. This can be explained by the little space available for pasture. In this context, the creation of sheep and goats was the most important. The specialized productions of Athens or Miletus, the center of wool production, were only isolated cases. Agricultural and livestock production units used both free and slave labor.

Aqueduct in Crete: the system was the basis of the water supply and helped the economy

WATER SUPPLY

The supply system in Ancient Greece consisted of aqueducts, a kind of trenches and tunnels used to transport water. The aqueduct of Eupalinos, in Samos, is considered one of the most impressive works of Greek antiquity. The city is actually an island, located in the Aegean Sea, which is about two kilometers off the coast of Turkey.

The Samos aqueduct is 1,036 meters long and crosses the Kastron mountain. It was built at the time of the tyrant Polycrates (550 BC). He was concerned about the water supply in the city, which had a growing population. The tunnel was opened so that water could be brought in from the spring of the Agiad fountain, which was on the other side of the mountain.

Another Greek invention that revolutionized the water supply system was the so-called Archimedes screw. He created this device, intended to take water from a lower level to a higher one, through the use of a tube with an internal screw. As the tube turned, the turns of the screw collected the water, pushing it into a storage tank. The screw was driven by human strength through the work of a slave who made it turn.

These inventions developed in Ancient Greece helped the economy and provided access to a more hygienic water supply.

THE TRADE AND THE SEA

The transport system in Ancient Greece was rudimentary and made even more difficult by the mountain ranges that separated the valleys. The Greeks transported their goods in many different ways. They employed oxen, horses, donkeys, and wagons. In extreme cases, the products were carried on the back.

There were still a few roads and bridges. To make things worse, robbers lay in wait on isolated mountain paths.

But if, on the one hand, the mountainous relief became an obstacle to certain Greek trade activities, geography helped the region in the consummation of maritime transactions. The jagged coastline and the large number of islands favored trade contacts by sea with the Greek colonies in Asia Minor, Sicily, cities along the Black Sea coast, and especially Egypt.

Through these transactions, the Greeks more often imported spices, wheat, flax, resin, papyrus – most of which came from the Egyptians – and wood. This closer contact of the Greeks with neighboring civilizations helped a lot in supplying the Greek city-states. In addition, they were determined to reduce agrarian conflicts, enriching these locations and their cultural expansion.

Within this development, the merchants of the Rhodes region instituted a system of maritime laws, which were later also adopted by the Romans. These laws formed the basis of all maritime legislation that would come into force later.

COINS

Even with the introduction of coins in the 6th century BC, it was maintained for a long time the use of direct exchange in the daily life of Ancient Greece, just as it occurs in simpler and less demanding markets, where there are relatively lower levels of productivity.

However, slowly, the product exchange system opened up more and more space for the monetary economy. Greek trade gained more dynamism with the adoption, by several city-states, of metal coins made of gold, silver, bronze, lead, and copper alloy, all classified as precious materials. The emergence of the coins is considered a major milestone in the economy of the time.

The technique of minting metal coins – the process by which the pieces are engraved – began approximately in the 6th century BC in the cities of Aegina and Athens. Images of heroes and gods worshiped by the Greeks were printed on them.

Coins not only served the population to sell and buy goods but were also used as a source of income. The first minting is attributed to the kingdom of Lydia, at the time of Croesus (around 547 BC), taking advantage of the territory's wide supply of gold.

ATHENIAN ECONOMY

During the 5th and 4th centuries BC, Athens was not only the largest but also the richest city in Ancient Greece. Reports show that the foreign trade volume – the sum of imports and exports from the cities of the Athenian Empire – amounted to 180 million Attic drachmas. As a comparison, this amount is twice as large as the government budget of the Persian Empire in the same historical period.

Maintaining slavery in Athens was the determining factor both for the development of the economy and for the consolidation of democracy, which enabled a more balanced political situation, since the popular layers of Athenian society had some of their claims met. With the preservation of slave labor, the economic elite continued to have a large amount of time available to participate in assemblies and other political activities.

Athens' development was also based on its leadership in the war against the Persians. Athenian military leadership and control over the wealth intended for battle increased production in the city, generated jobs, balanced the economy, and created conditions for imposing dominion over other Greek cities.

GREEK MERCHANT SHIPS

Greek traders used small wooden ships to transport their products. Merchant ships had no decks and were driven by oars and sails. In several places, these ships were pulled over narrow strips of land on special tracks.

They differed from war vessels, very narrow wooden ships with metal prows, which were used as battering rams – war machines used to breach walls or gates of fortresses. In winter, trade and transport almost completely ceased in Ancient Greece, as snow and storms blocked land routes and made the sea very dangerous.

8

DECLINE OF ATHENS AND THE CITY-STATES

INTERNAL DISPUTES, LIKE THE PERSIAN AND PELOPONNESIAN WARS, WERE THE STARTING POINT FOR THE DEFEAT OF THE GREEK EMPIRE BY THE MACEDONIANS

The Hellenistic period is an important phase in the history of Ancient Greece and part of the Middle East, which began in 336 BC – the year of the advancement of Alexander the Great from Macedonia – and ended in the 1ˢᵗ century BC, when Egypt, the last Hellenistic kingdom, was annexed by the Roman Empire. This moment was a milestone between the dominance of Greek culture and the emergence of Roman civilization.

At that time, there was a clear decrease in the relevance of the current territory of Greece within the Greek-speaking region. So much so that the two main centers of Hellenistic culture were Antioch, the capital of Seleucid Syria, and Alexandria, the capital of Ptolemaic Egypt. There were other important centers as well, but they were all located outside mainland Greece. These were the cases, for example, of Smyrna, Ephesus, Pergamum, and Seleucia on Tigris.

The Hellenistic period was notable, mainly, for the development of science and knowledge. Syria, Macedonia, and Egypt are the most directly impacted. Later, with the advancement of Rome, the three kingdoms are absorbed by the new power, opening space for the time that marks the end of Antiquity.

THE MACEDONIAN ADVANCEMENT

The importance of Greek territory, not its culture, started being undermined after the Persian and Peloponnesian wars, which

Gold coin features the face of the king of Macedonia, Philip II

helped to weaken the city-states. These two battles annihilated part of the small populations, the localities had their infrastructure destroyed, and consequently, trade and agricultural activities were extremely impaired. In addition to these human and economic losses, the conflicts seriously affected the military contingent that was on standby to protect Greece from possible foreign invasions.

Thus, the monarch of Macedonia, Philip II, saw in the Greek decline an excellent opportunity to conquer the city-states. The Macedonian territory was located to the north of Greece, on a strip of land considered quite small. The population was basically composed of descendants of the primitive Greeks, who survived from grazing and also from agriculture.

The reality is that Macedonia's modernization process began with Philip II himself. He took power in 356 BC and has since implemented several internal reforms. Knowing the rivalries that existed between the Greek states, Philip II started outlining the conquest of Greece. In 338 BC, he overcame the Greeks in the so- called Battle of Chaeronea. However, shortly after, in 336 BC, the king died.

The throne was assumed by the son of Philip II, Alexander the Great, who controls the Greek uprising that started after his father's death. At that time, it gained huge strength from his plan to conquer the East. The project, by the way, was not new. The Greeks themselves already dreamed of taking the Persian treasures for themselves, in revenge for the attacks of Darius and Xerxes, and expanding their territorial domain beyond the Aegean Sea.

At just 20 years old, Alexander the Great became Emperor. He was considered a great military man and one of the greatest warriors of antiquity. Quite young, only 18 years old, he distinguished himself as the commander of one of the wings of the Macedonian army in the Battle of Chaeronea itself.

But Alexander did not only demonstrate resourcefulness in wars. He was also endowed with an excellent potential for intellect, among other reasons, because he had a creation based on Greek culture. He had been educated by Aristotle, one of the main philosophers of Ancient Greece. He also had contact with eastern culture through the many people that made up the Macedonian domain. As emperor, he managed to surpass not only the works of his father but those of almost all the monarchs of the East.

THE REBELLION OF THEBES

Because of Alexander's young age, the Greeks believed that liberation would not be difficult. However, they were underestimating the capacity of the young emperor.

In 335 BC, when the king had just returned from his pursuit of the Illyrians, the first information reached him about a revolutionary movement in Thebes with the help of Athens. The exiles, upon their return to the city at the invitation of their supporters, had murdered two innocent Macedonians from the garrison. They then spread the word that Alexander had died in Illyria and persuaded the Thebans to rise for freedom.

Soon, the emperor realized that the rebellion could be quite dangerous. He had been suspicious of cities like Athens, Sparta, and Aetolia for some time. So, he marched so quickly with the imperial army toward Thebes that the local people were not even aware of his approach.

Upon arriving there, Alexander still waited a little longer before attacking, as he expected them to surrender. However, the Thebans decided to attack the Macedonian camp and killed some soldiers.

Even with the onslaught of the rebels, Alexander still delayed the attacks, which, in the end, would have resulted in the deaths of 6,000 and the capture of another 30,000 people.

According to historians, the defeat of the Macedonians would have come in just two days. The king ordered the almost total destruction of the city, leaving intact only the residence where the Greek poet Pindar, extremely admired by Alexander, had lived.

THE EXPANSION OF THE MACEDONIAN TERRITORY

Faced with frustrated attempts by the colonized Greeks to rise, Alexander the Great worked even harder to extend his domain. He left toward Africa and Asia. He went on and conquered part of In-

DID YOU KNOW?

Contrary to what one might imagine, the term "Hellenism" was used for the first time only in the 19th century, by Joham Gustav Droysen, a German historian. The meaning of the word refers to the idea of "living like the Greeks."

dia, the whole Persian empire, Phoenicia, and also Egypt. He still had in his heart the desire to supplant the cities that extended into the Ganges River region. History tells, however, that his soldiers were already exhausted in the face of several consecutive battles and did not want to proceed with the emperor's plan.

Even without the annexation of these other lands, Macedonia had already become the core of one of the greatest domains in the ancient world: the Empire of Alexander.

CULTURAL INTEGRATION

The clearest proof of Alexander the Great's intelligence was his ability to manage such an eclectic environment. As emperor, he decided to respect different religions and political institutions. In addition, he encouraged marriage between winners and losers. The emperor also allowed young Persians to participate in the Greco-Macedonian armies. Another tactic used was the fusion between people, aiming to end disputes and inequalities between each of them.

In this way, he sought to set up a propitious scenario for cultural integration within the huge conquered empire. As the most outstanding result of this long work, the Hellenistic culture emerged, originating from the fusion of Greek (or Hellenic) culture with the Eastern one.

DEATH OF ALEXANDER AND THE DIVISION

The cause of the death of Alexander the Great in 323 BC, in Babylon, still raises some discussion. Some believe that the emperor contracted malaria. However, other historians claim that the death seems to be much more related to what has been called the West Nile virus. Alexander would have been affected by a very high fever caused by an infection. There is another more curious theory, which states that his death was caused by a serious intestinal disorder.

In any case, it resulted in deep changes in the Macedonian Empire. Internal struggles became constant, and the conquered territory was divided among several generals. In this way, three great kingdoms were formed: Syria (composed of Syria, Asia Minor, Mesopotamia, and Persia); Egypt (which encompassed

City of Corinth, where Flaminius announced a "false freedom" to Greek cities

Egypt, Phoenicia, and Palestine); and Macedonia (encompassed by Macedonia and Greece).

Such divisions generated particularities in some sectors. In politics, the new empires adopted customs from the eastern monarchies. In the economy, new trade routes were opened, and there was an expansion of the circulation of spices and luxury products, which were also spread in the West. Cities such as Alexandria, Antioch, and Pergamum became major centers for the production of ceramics, fabrics, metallurgy, and shipbuilding. In the cultural field, there were quite significant changes: the Greek tradition merged with the eastern ones – Babylonian, Egyptian, and Persian –, giving rise to the Hellenistic culture.

UPRISINGS AND CONFEDERACIES

The news of Alexander the Great's death inflamed the city of Athens and also its allies (the populations of Central Greece and the Peloponnese, except Sparta). An uprising against Macedonia was then organized, but the defeat of the rebels occurred in just one year, in the Lamian War.

The divisions established in the Macedonian Empire placed Greece, Thrace, and Anatolia under the Antigonid dynasty, which was a group of Hellenic kings who descended from Antigonus Monophthalmus, a general of Alexander's army. Other city-state rebellions were also recorded during this time of Macedonian control. Pergamum, Rhodes, Athens, and certain Greek states joined the Aetolian League (or Aetolian Confederacy) in order to defend the flag of independence.

The Achaean Confederacy was, in theory, subject to the Ptolemaic dynasty, which dominated the territory of Egypt after the death of Alexander the Great. However, this League controlled most of southern Greece and acted in a way that was quite independent. On the other hand, Sparta, despite also moving towards independence, refused to be part of any confederacy.

In the year 267 BC, the then king of Egypt, Ptolemy II, managed to persuade the Greek cities to rise against Macedonia, which originated the Chremonidean War, named after the Athenian leader Chremonides. However, the Greeks suffered a new defeat, and Athens consequently lost its independence and democratic institutions. The setback brought an end to Athens' era as a strong and influential political agent of antiquity. However, the city remained the largest and richest in all of Greece.

Twelve years later, in 255 BC, Macedonia led a resounding victory over the Egyptian fleet on the island of Kos and increased its dominance over all other Aegean islands, except for Rhodes.

In turn, Sparta continued to be an enemy of the Achaeans. Thus, in 227 BC, it ended up invading Achaia and taking control of that confederacy. The remaining Achaeans decided to distance themselves once and for all from Macedonia and have Sparta as their main ally. But in 222 BC, Macedonian troops overcame the Spartan army and annexed the city. This was the first time that Sparta had been occupied by a foreign power.

Philip V of Macedonia was the last Greek ruler to dispose of the talent and also the opportunity to try to unite Greece as a whole and preserve its independence in the face of Roman power and the consequent threat of a war of extermination. In 201 BC, a peace pact ended conflicts between Macedonia and the Greek confederacies. At that moment, Philip V already had control of almost all of Greece, except Athens, Rhodes, and Pergamum.

THE MACEDONIAN WARS

Two years after the peace agreement, Philip would forge an agreement of union with Carthage, the enemy of Rome. Instantly, the Romans worked to seduce the Achaean cities and gained the support they needed. Achaia abandoned loyalty to Philip. Rome also made important alliances with Rhodes and Pergamum, considered the main powers in Asia Minor.

It did not take long for the tension to rise. The First Macedonian War broke out in 214 BC and lasted until 205 BC, but there was no declared victorious side. Even so, the Macedonians were deeply marked as Roman enemies.

In 202 BC, Rome ruthlessly defeated Carthage. After the victory, its eyes turned to the East. Then, in 198 BC, the Second Macedonian War broke out. The reasons were quite obscure, but the reality is that the Romans saw Macedonia as a potential ally of the Seleucids, who represented the greatest eastern power at the time.

BATTLE OF CYNOSCEPHALAE

In Greece, Philip lost his allies, who deserted. In 197 BC, he was finally defeated by the Roman consul, Titus Quinctius Flaminius, at the Battle of Cynoscephalae. But the Greeks had the sympathy of Flaminius, known as a very moderate man and, moreover, a confessed admirer of Greek culture. The fact that he knew and spoke the Greek language, by the way, caused many of Philip's allies to defect to Flaminius' side. Thus, Philip also needed to ally himself with the Romans to be spared.

FALSE FREEDOM

In 196 BC, during the Isthmian Games, a festival in honor of Poseidon, the god of the sea, in Corinth, Flaminius declared, to the effusive enthusiasm of all, the independence of the Greek cities. In theory, although the Roman garrisons are still among the Corinthians and in Chalcidice, the localities would be free.

THE ROMAN MILITARY DOMINANCE

Greece had entered into a total decline in its military forces. Thus, the Romans did not have to make so much effort to conquer all the territory.

The beginning of Rome's rule over the Greeks is conventionally dated back to the sack of Corinth in 146 BC by Lucius Mummius. However, Macedonia had already fallen under Roman control in 168 BC, with the defeat of King Perseus in the city of Pydna.

From that moment on, the Romans divided the region into four smaller republics. In 146 BC, Macedonia was already a Roman province, which made Thessalonica its capital. The other Greek city-states gradually also buried their autonomy and succumbed to Rome. Even so, the Romans kept local administration in the hands of the Greeks themselves and did not seek to intervene in the long-institutionalized pattern of traditional politics. Thus, the agora in Athens remained the center of civil and cultural life.

Greece remained part of the eastern half of Rome's domain, which would later become the so-called Byzantine Empire. The Greek peninsula, by the way, would have been one of the most developed regions of the Roman Empire. According to historians, it continued to prosper until at least the 6th century BC because of the tradition of urban development in the Greek East.

GREEK CULTURE CONQUERS THE EMPIRE

If, militarily, the Romans showed their superiority, on the other hand, Greek culture had also won its supporters. Despite the closure of an era, some aspects of Hellenism remained in the Roman Empire for many years.

So much so that in the region of Palestine, also dominated by the Romans, despite Aramaic being the popular language in the first century, skilled Jewish traders used the Greek language to serve their customers well and sell their goods. Another clear case of Hellenistic influence is the New Testament, which was written in a popular strain of Greek: Koine.

This enduring cultural influence can be explained by the fact that the Romans themselves were dominated by the Greeks and subjected to Hellenism earlier. Thus, the culture of Ancient Greece was perpetuated by the Roman Empire.

9

THE ADVANCEMENT OF GRECO-ROMAN IDEAS

THE CUSTOMS AND THOUGHTS OF THE TWO PEOPLE ARE MERGED AND INFLUENCE THE WEST

*Ancient engravings of Greek letters in rock: the language
was studied by the Romans during the Empire*

At first sight, the rise of the Roman Empire could mean the homogenization of the cultures of the dominated localities. The militarily strongest would impose their habits. However, that was not quite what happened. At least with regard to Ancient Greece. Physically slaughtered by the Romans, the Greeks are known to have culturally influenced the owners of the new Empire.

According to the Latin poet Horace (1st century BC), "captured Greece conquered the proud conqueror." A very clear proof of this is that the gods and their incredible stories were practically all incorporated by the Romans. Their names, in general, were translated. Zeus, for example, became Jupiter. Aphrodite became Venus, and Poseidon became Neptune.

The entire southern region of the Italian Peninsula and Sicily were colonized by the Greek people, and thus, Magna Graecia was formed. In addition, the Romans coexisted with the Greeks for several centuries. Even the stories of Rome were embedded in Greek mythology.

According to historians, the best explanation for this influence of the Greeks is the fact that, when two cultures meet, the one that is superior manages to impose itself in relation to the other. This would also explain the so-called Europeanization of the world.

Thus, the cultural superiority of Greece would be the determining factor for the occurrence of the process that culminated in the adoption by the Romans of Greek values, customs, and ideals. This event is called Hellenization.

However, another point of view emphasizes that the reason for the absorption would not be this Greek prominence in relation to culture, but rather the ability of the Roman people to adapt and transform customs and thoughts different from their own.

It is noteworthy that the Roman elite studied Greek, spoke the Hellenic language, and wrote it perfectly. In addition, it collected works of art from Greece. However, the curious thing is that they kept a certain distance from the colonized. A Roman saying from that time warned: "Beware of the Greeks."

Vladimir Wrangel/ Shutterstock.com

*Sculpture with the image of
Jupiter in Rome, Italy*

HELLENIZATION

The undeniable fact is that, after the conquest of Greek territory in the 2nd century BC, the Romans underwent a very marked change in their habits. That great civilization began to be studied more deeply by the citizens of Rome. Not only the language of Greece, but also the literature and its admired philosophy. Not only were pieces of art commissioned but Greek teachers also started being sought by the Romans. Athens maintained its status as a university city, where the Romans went to complete their education in philosophy and rhetoric.

Over time, the more affluent inhabitants of the ruling nation even knew the Greek language better than Latin. As a parallel, it can be said that the difference in importance between the two languages at the time was the same as that between English and Portuguese today.

Interestingly, the Greeks, although overcome by the conquerors, did not show much concern with learning Latin. On the other hand, the Romans started using Greek in everything that was published in the Hellenic-speaking world. It is important to remember that in Macedonia, Peloponnese, Asia Minor, Syria, Palestine, and

EMPEROR MARCUS AURELIUS AND HIS "MEDITATIONS"

The Greek influence in the formation of the Roman emperor Marcus Aurelius was immortalized through a notebook of personal writings that he, at the time, had titled only "to myself." However, such notes were gathered and formed, sometime later, posthumously, the work "Meditations."

The set of 12 books brings many maxims about Marcus Aurelius' self-knowledge and personal development. In that work, he says, for example, that "the only way a man can be dominated by others is to allow his own reaction to take hold of him." Another reflection says that "an order or logos permeates the universe" and that "rationality and a clear mind allow us to live in harmony with this logos."

Despite having faced some wars and making several persecutions, Marcus Aurelius owned an administration famous for success and peace. He is rated as one of the "Five Good Roman Emperors," along with Nerva, Trajan, Hadrian, and Antoninus Pius.

In addition, he was considered a stoic and extremely cultured philosopher. His work, "Meditations," is compared with other highly esteemed literature, such as the "Confessions," by St. Augustine. Former US President Bill Clinton had "Meditations" as one of his bedside books.

Egypt, Greek was the official language of the Empire. In addition, even considering themselves Romans over the years, the Greeks did not cease to be Greeks either, with their customs and language remaining intact.

Given this scenario, the city of Rome became the newest and most important center of Hellenic culture. There, medicine and the teaching of philosophy and rhetoric, so prized by the Romans, were in the hands of the Greeks. Even the Roman emperors themselves revered ancient Greek culture. Among all, Nero, Hadrian, and Marcus Aurelius are considered the most notable.

ROME: A CULTURAL MELTING POT

Interestingly, the other conquered peoples – at least most of them – did not enjoy such high respect from Rome. These inhabitants continued to use their languages and quietly practiced their customs. However, only Latin was allowed, in practice, as the official language of communication.

For centuries, different languages – such as Celtic in Gaul, Egyptian in Egypt, and Aramaic in Palestine – continued to be used by the populations of those regions. Nor did the Welsh speak Latin.

But as time went by, there was a severe transformation in the Roman world. All those different people ended up mixing, thoughts and customs were mixed, and syncretism took over a good part of that region. Ideas and values were mixed up, and there was constant interaction.

THE PILLARS OF GREEK THINKING

There are many aspects that helped to perpetuate the Greek way of thinking. In a Greco-Roman environment, such ideas entered the process of transformation but did not lose their essence. Those responsible for these strong pillars were three: Socrates, Plato, and Aristotle, who lived between the 5th and 4th centuries BC.

Concepts such as the "birth of ideas" (Socrates), the "division between the spiritual plane and the physical plane" (Plato), and the "imitation of reality with the aim of seeking perfection" (Aristotle) formed the basis of thinking and questioning that would leave a legacy for Western culture more than 2 thousand years later.

So long after, we continue to be inspired by their realistic sculpture, to represent their theater, and to discuss democracy as a form of government. In addition, the languages and the Latin- based model of Christianity remain laden with countless Greek values, terms, and images.

THE GRECO-ROMAN SOCIETY

Knowing the aspects of the Roman Empire is essential for understanding this plural society because even after all the transformations that took place in this civilization over time, some characteristics were maintained, even if this always brought a new look.

However, two considerable social divisions remained almost intact: that of citizens and non-citizens and that of free and unfree.

In general terms, the free ones were divided into two groups: those of free birth and former slaves. The first ones could be Roman citizens or non-citizens, as citizens had rights not available to other classes.

In this way, Roman society was, at the same time, known for its divisions and for the possibility of mobility within that scale. That is, a slave had the chance to stop being a slave, and a non- citizen could become a citizen. Another alternative was for a slave to re-

This painting depicts conversation between slave and his masters

ceive manumission and its child to become a citizen. As a citizen, it would have the right, for example, to be elected to exercise a magistracy function. Contrary to what we might think, cases like this happened with some frequency.

In the period when the great territorial conquests took place, Rome also used to classify citizens in orders or groupings. These divisions were made not only by material wealth but also by social recognition. Such separations remained in the Greco-Roman culture.

HELLENISM AND CHRISTIANITY

In 391 AC, the Roman Empire adopted Christianity as its official religion. In this way, so-called pagan cults were prohibited. Even so, classical culture remained very important and active. This was possible thanks to religious syncretism. Mainly in the most influential social circles, texts by Aristotle and Plato gain prominence – and even by Roman authors such as Virgil, writer of the epopee "Aeneid."

Within this religious context, the Christian culture overlapped the classical one, which had its pagan base reformulated with new shapes and contours. However, the permanence of some aspects of Greek culture was conditioned by the rules of Christian dogmas. Only practices that do not come into direct conflict with the doctrines of Christianity, a monotheistic universe, would be accepted.

Thus, in 394 AC, the Olympic Games were prohibited, as they were seen by the church and consequently by the State as a pagan cult. The fact that its origin was linked to the several gods of Gre-

BREAD AND CIRCUS

Despite this scenario of social mobility, the success of the conquests and the heavy use of slave labor significantly increased the number of commoners – poor citizens – without occupation in the Roman Empire. These were joined by small farmers, who had their crops ruined and also moved from the countryside to the cities.

Thus, the most urbanized areas became swollen, mainly the capital. In an attempt to reduce the problem of the mass of unemployed people living in Rome, the state decided to pay them subsidies. Thus, the poorest received food at low prices and also could watch free public shows for fun. The "bread and circus policy" was established.

co-Roman mythology confronted the first fruits of worship to a single god, the Christian. So much so that the Olympics were only resumed in the modern era, in 1894, through the creation of the IOC (International Olympic Committee) by the French educator Pierre de Frédy, the famous Baron de Coubertin (1863-1937). The first edition of the Modern Games would take place two years later in the city of Athens, in 1896.

In addition to the closure of the Olympic Games, in 529 AD, the schools of philosophy in Athens were closed by order of Emperor Justinian. Many claim that this fateful year marked the end of the creative vigor of ancient Greek culture.

BIBLICAL NARRATIVES AND THE INFLUENCES OF THE EMPIRE

According to biblical accounts, in Palestine, dominated by the Roman Empire, Jesus and his disciples communicated in Aramaic in everyday life and their religion was in no way related to Roman beliefs. The four gospels that tell the story of the carpenter from Nazareth – Matthew, Mark, Luke, and John – were written in Greek. On the other hand, Jesus did not preach either in Latin or in the Hellenic language.

Interestingly, there is only one known phrase of Jesus in his usual language, Aramaic. This sentence was said at the moment of his death: "Eloí, Eloí, lama sabachthani?" Translating: "My God, my God, why have you forsaken me?" (Mark 15.39).

Reports like these show that the possibilities of communication, already at that time, were diverse.

In addition, the Christian holy book also shows that a good social condition – read financial success – allowed Roman citizenship to be achieved, including by foreigners of the Empire. This is what the dialogue between the apostle Paul, a Jewish rabbi from the city of Tarsus and speaker of the Greek language, with a Roman commander shows. "As they were tying him up in order to flog him, Paul said to the centurion standing there, 'Do you have the right to flog a Roman citizen without him being condemned?' Upon hearing this, the centurion went to warn the commander: 'What are you going to do? This man is a Roman citizen'. The commander went up to Paul and asked, 'Tell me, are you a Roman citizen?' He replied, 'Yes, I am'. Then the commander said: 'I had to pay a high price for my citizenship'. Paul replied, 'I have it by birthright'." (Acts 22:25-28).

WOMEN IN GRECO-ROMAN SOCIETY

Prejudice against women was quite noticeable in the Greco-Roman period. Men classified them as more fragile beings whose main function was to generate children in order to guarantee the continuity of the human race. They were also supposed to "provide" her husband with pleasure and carry out her household tasks. This line of thinking ended up permeating Western culture.

Women did not have any voting rights in Greek and Roman assemblies, which were the policymaking events of society at the time. This is because they did not have active citizenship.

They were classified into three types: wives, concubines, and prostitutes. The first ones were those that remained restricted to the family environment. In this way, there was no contact with other males, except those who made up their own family. Concubines, in turn, were women – both slaves and free – who assisted their masters in day-to-day tasks. Prostitutes or courtesans – at that time, also called "she-wolves" by the Romans – were seen as the main source of pleasure, thus preserving the purity of free women (the wives and daughters of citizens).

The brothels of that period were popularly called "lupanars." The women who worked in these brothels were separated according to

Painting shows sexual intercourse between prostitute and Roman citizen

their beauty. Philosophers and artists often enjoyed these passions. They generally said that they looked for "inspiration" in them.

However, it is important to highlight that, with regard to wives, husbands carried the responsibility of ensuring them respect and protection. If the husband died, for example, they would lose this condition, and could end up in complete poverty. In several cases, these women would need to resort to prostitution to survive.

GASTRONOMY

The fusion of the two cultures also reached the tables of the inhabitants of the Roman Empire. There was a period of exchanging different products from different parts of the world. The diet consisted basically of fruits and vegetables. The population consumed a lot of onions, garlic, turnips, pomegranates, oranges, and grapes.

The Greeks brought to the Roman dish a typical food that had barley as its main element. It was a kind of porridge that, when consumed in a more refined way, also contained wine and animal brains.

In fact, only noble citizens ate meat from different types of animals, with the exception of beef cuts, because they had the ox as an alternative to animal traction.

The Mediterranean also allowed the consumption of countless species of fish and seafood. The capital, Rome, helped spread the use of spices such as parsley, oregano, and pepper.

A significant quantity and variety of breads were produced. In the beginning, it was a task exclusively for women. However, from the third century, the first bakers and bread houses started appearing. There were first, second, and third quality breads. This latter, as one might figure, was consumed by the poorest strata. Most often, bread was eaten with spices, eggs, and figs.

As it is a grape-producing region, it is not surprising that wine was present at most of the feasts. The Romans started dominating, over the years, many wine conservation techniques. However, there were also other quite common drinks, such as posca, made from vinegar and water (the poorest people and soldiers were the main consumers); zhytum, a beer made from barley or wheat; and camum, also produced from barley, but which went through the fermentation process.

GASTRONOMIC LEGACY

This period guaranteed a legacy in the technical evolution of gastronomy. At that time, cauldrons were created; pans were no longer made of clay, which guaranteed greater safety for cooks; stoves left public places and moved to private spaces; elements of table etiquette emerged (use of forks, spoons, and napkins); and towels started being used on the tables.

THE FASHION

Classical Greek and Roman clothing had curious characteristics. The garment was folded, rolled, and attached to the body with a clip. This was because, at the time, fabrics were considered too precious to be wasted on cutting or modeling.

The clothes had a very large number of pleats and folds. Among the Romans, the costume had two more common combinations of pieces: a tunic with a palla – a rectangle of fabric over the stole – for women and a tunic with a toga for men.

Tunics were worn closer to the body. Their format alternated greatly according to a person's activity, class, or gender. The material had a direct relationship with the status of the citizen. The name of the male version of the garment was chiton, which, over time, came to be worn at knee length.

In turn, the tunic worn by women had a longer length and was called peplos. Both forms of the tunic were made up of a large rectangle of fabric folded over the body and secured with clasps.

The Ionian chiton, a piece of wealthier citizens, was made of the finest fabric, such as silk or linen. The Doric chiton, the simplest model, was made of wool. The semi-permanent pleats were obtained by ironing and pressing the fabric under the heat of the sun. The chiton worn by slaves and commoners basically consisted of two rectangles joined by a seam, with a hole at the top and a hole at the bottom, for the head, arms, and legs.

Higher status men wore garments decorated with vertical stripes. It is noteworthy that the sumptuary laws were very strict, and there were regulations on who could or could not wear each type of clothing.

The tunic worn by women was looser and was worn with a belt under the chest, waist and hips. In addition, more sophisticated models were found, with sleeves finished off at the wrist by means of a strip of more rigid fabric. These tunics left the arms on display.

In the environment of the Roman Empire, garments known in Greece as "himation" could also be worn over tunics – for dignity or to protect against the weather. It was a unisex cape worn by men, often without the tunic underneath. Soldiers were in the habit of wearing another type of cape, called "chlamys," which was shorter.

The toga was a very common garment in Ancient Rome. Wrapped around the body, it had a short, rectangular shape. Over time, it became semicircular, and its size increased: it reached an incredible six meters on the straight side. It was such a difficult garment to wear, so much so that the wealthier Romans had a slave only to help carry the tail of the toga.

Foreigners and servants were prohibited from wearing the toga, a trademark of Roman citizens. Clothing was evidence not only of material possessions but also of social importance.

The children born freed indicated their condition amid society by means of a white toga with a purple stripe. However, the toga con-

Illustration brings details of male and female clothing in the Roman Empire

sidered the most opulent was the picta, which was vastly decorated, purple in color, embroidered in gold, and dressed by emperors.

The Romans also wore a toga called pulla, a dark garment specially made for times of mourning.

ARCHITECTURE

Greco-Roman architecture had a direct influence on the cultural and artistic evolution of the West. The ancient Greeks created several works of art, for example, for temples and public buildings. As the Olympic religion of Greece beckoned to gods with human forms, there was the conception of images of idols, which soon needed adequate shelter. These places were erected in the form of houses.

In the so-called Dark Ages, residences could have a circular, elliptical, or rectangular shape. With that, the temples would logically assume one of these forms. It was then that the rectangle prevailed.

However, the main increment of Greek architecture happened when the columns were placed around the temple building. Within this context, three norms of architectural composition developed in Greece: Doric, Ionic, and Corinthian.

These evolutions in classical Greek architecture directly influenced other people at the time of their creation. The Romans adopted columns and other Greek shapes as basis and made adaptations in their own way. In other locations, the exuberant Greek architectural style ended up being used in more personal constructions, such as the houses themselves.

Despite being considered a derivation of Greek architecture, the Roman strand also generated its own characteristics and left a vast collection for the West. The buildings of that time can be found all over Europe and are still the object of study today.

However, the importance of architecture in Rome is not restricted to beauty and aesthetics. The very high quality of the construction is impressive. The Pantheon, for example, remains in good condition even after so long. The architecture of Ancient Rome is so excellent that certain techniques from that period are still being used, such as the aqueducts that supply water to some villages. Currently, architecture professionals have sought to combine those ancient elements with new concepts. What is impressive is that these legacies are not restricted to decoration, but also

TRADITION OF BREAKING DISHES

During this period, the Greeks maintained the curious habit of breaking dishes. It is not clear how this idea came about, but historians say it had been embedded in Greek culture for 4,000 years. Some believe that one of the possible explanations for this tradition would be that the inhabitants of Ancient Greece believed that breaking utensils warded off evil spirits. In addition, it would be proof of detachment from material goods.

In modern times, such an action started having other meanings and was used by the public to show satisfaction for an artist or to cheer up people who were dancing. Much later, already in the 1930s, breaking dishes had already become such a normal practice that restaurants were used to buying ceramics especially for them to be broken at the end of the night.

Currently, the tradition is prohibited in Greek restaurants because of the high number of people who end up getting hurt by the pieces of the dishes. To fill this gap, the custom was exchanged for another one: now the Greeks throw flowers.

to better structuring.

In the southern United States, the influence of Greek architecture is quite noticeable in Greek Renaissance-style homes. Some residences use magnificent columns. There are also small terraced houses with columns at the entrances.

In contemporary public and government buildings there is also an evident reference. All because Greek architecture projects authority, permanence, and power, essential qualities for such buildings. The Supreme Court of the United States is a case in point. It presents concepts of Corinthian architecture. The west entrance has 16 Corinthian columns under a carved architrave. These columns are topped with a wreath of acanthus leaves with meticulously engraved details.

Use of columns is one of the main characteristics of Greek architecture

10

THE EVOLUTION OF ARTISTIC EXPRESSIONS

THE GREEKS PERFECTED THE ART OF THE EGYPTIANS AND PROVIDED IMPORTANT ADVANCEMENTS IN CULTURAL PRODUCTION

By the time they arrived in the Peloponnese from the north, the Greeks were considered individuals of different tribes and not a people in itself. This is due to the fact that they spoke different dialects and are governed by different leaders. Among them, the best-known groups were the Ionians, Dorians, and Aeolians. Later, however, already spread over the most varied areas of the Peninsula, the Greeks originated a civilization recognized as one of the most magnificent of ancient times.

When they maintained contact with the Phoenicians, they developed activities such as trade and navigation, and also learned writing. The inhabitants of Greece, especially those of Athens, were known to be very curious, dynamic, and avid for novelties.

Such predicates were fundamental for them to be able to produce an unprecedented type of art and culture. They cultivated an especially rich mythology and masterfully developed philosophy, theater, and sports revolutions, the main event being the Olympic Games, held every four years in honor of Zeus (the main god of Greek mythology). These ancient conceptions make up the cultural treasure of humanity to this day.

Artistic production in almost all Greek territory came to be called Mycenaean art. The exception was Crete, where the Minoan style was developed. In general, Greek artists sought to manifest what they found in nature itself. They sought to express their works with perfection, harmony, and balance.

After a phase of frank influence from Mesopotamia, Greek art knew a fertile and mature time, in the archaic period, which lasted until 475 BC. The basis of the artistic production that would follow was laid at that moment when its aesthetic pillars were defined.

After confronting the Persians on the battlefields, Greek art achieved an important conquest: its cultural autonomy in the Mediterranean region. The so-called classical phase lasted from 475 BC to 323 BC and constituted the last essentially Greek artistic period. This is called the golden age of its artistic movement, led by the city of Athens.

THE PRINCIPLE OF GREEK ART

The beginning of the artistic activities of those people also presented rustic and somewhat primitive works. Even so, the way was already laid out for a style that, gradually being polished, would become a great example and would come to be admired for several years and different people.

The art of the Greeks, as well as that of the Egyptians, was also built for their gods or regarding them. The difference, however, was that these deities had human forms, and the sacred temples built for them did not have the magnificent dimensions of the buildings in Egypt. In addition, there was no "divine" ruler so powerful as to enslave and force people to work for him.

SCULPTURES

The tribes of Greece were spread over numerous cities, including the so-called "city-states." However, despite a certain rivalry between them, none exerted absolute dominance over the others.

As the art historian Ernst Hans Josef Gombrich wrote, it was in Athens that the "greatest and most astonishing revolution in the whole history of art borne its fruit." Where and on what date is not exactly known. What is known is that Greek artists began this process by making stone statues, a continuation of the work of the Egyptians. In this period, there was a certain balance between fol-

An ancient painted Greek amphora

lowing certain rules and freedom of creation. Without exception, Greek sculptors wanted to understand how to represent a given body. While the Egyptians based their art on knowledge, the Greeks started using their own eyes. Then this revolution began.

There are very clear traces of Egyptian art in the works produced by the Greeks, who, however, were more interested in their own experiences. They were no longer worried with following the consecrated rules of yesteryear.

In the statues of the brothers Kleobis and Biton, produced by Polymedes, it is possible to verify several Egyptian norms. On the other hand, there is also a search for innovation; the knees are marked with the aim of reproducing them as they really are. This sculptor began his own experimentation. He could have followed the Egyptian knee shape, as he did in most forms, but he was concerned with doing it differently, experimenting with another way of representing the figure, even if this experience resulted in a solution that was not as good as that of his colleagues from the Nile.

Thus, discoveries and new ideas gradually emerged. The sculptor tried some innovative techniques and immediately shared them

Bust of Nefertiti, Egyptian piece from 1360 BC: Egypt influenced Greek art

Statues of Kleobis and Biton by the Greek sculptor Polymedes

with others. Through exchange, artists added their own skills and innovations to what they received from others.

An important aspect to point out is that the Greeks did not aim or intend to represent in their pieces the best vision of what would be portrayed. They preferred to face the challenge of presenting things as they saw them.

These Greek artists no longer felt rooted or forced to show everything that passed in front of them. They no longer considered all those forms of representation so sacred. Even with the rules, they had the freedom to create with more detachment. Sculptors could only represent a piece of a hand when it was behind the other hand. In short, for these Greek explorers and artists, the study of a shape was of utmost importance. Understanding and being able to represent the shape were their challenges.

In this context, they explored the anatomy of bones and also muscles, even though they were representing the figure with clothing. The draped garment followed the shape of the body, not simply covering it. The clothing, in a way, revealed the body.

Thus, these artists created figures that impressed everybody. It is true that the first works did not have all the vigor they achieved later on. However, the quest for form perfection was already notable. Perhaps the portraits also did not bring the person portrayed to mind, but there was an intention to imitate the real face. They produced them according to their knowledge of the human figure, in its best form.

THE SEARCH FOR THE IDEAL FIGURE

When sculpting, the Greeks sought perfection, with man as the main theme. Thus, human beings and their behavior on different occasions were portrayed. In the same way, their gods were created. The sculpture "Apollo Belvedere" shows the ideal Greek model of a man's body. Today, the difficulty in identifying certain traces of Greek works occurs because the statues that we know are, in large part, copies produced by the Romans. Thanks to these replicas, we can get an idea of what the Greek pieces were like, but these copies have a slightly more delicate appearance compared to the originals.

One of the most important sculptors of that period, Phidias, was responsible not only for the decoration of the Parthenon but also for

STATUES DESTROYED IN THE CHRISTIAN PERIOD

The Austrian historian Ernst Hans Josef Gombrich explains in his book, *The History of Art*, that the reason for the disappearance of almost all the statues of the ancient world was that, after the rise of Christianity, already in the Roman Empire, "it was considered pious to destroy statues of pagan gods."

the statue of Zeus in Olympia, two of his main works. This 11-metre-tall statue was lost, but fragments were found in the temple of Zeus in Olympia and still exist.

MOVEMENT

In addition to Phidias, another very relevant artist of this period was Myron, who incorporated movement into sculpture. Frequent requests for "statues in action" may have helped sculptors like him perfect their skills and knowledge of the human body in full motion.

The interest in pieces "in action" was linked to sports. A temple like the one at Olympia was continually surrounded by statues of victorious athletes dedicated to mythological gods. This may sound strange nowadays, as it is not expected, no matter how popular they are, to see images of our champions offered to a church as thanks for a conquered victory.

However, the great sports meetings of the Greeks, of which the Olympic Games were the noblest, had very different characteristics from our modern competitions. They were more closely linked to the religious beliefs and rites of the people.

Those who participated in the games were not simple sportsmen – amateurs or professionals – but members of the main families of Greece. The winners of these competitions were viewed with veneration. They were thought to be men whom the gods had favored with the gift of invincibility.

It was to find out to whom the blessing of victory fell that they originally held the games. To celebrate and perhaps perpetuate this sign of divine grace, the winners commissioned their statues from the most famous artists of the period.

Each in their own time, Greek sculptors were increasingly achieving the desired "perfection" in their works. Their concern was to represent what they saw with perfect movements, faces, and bodies.

More than that, they managed to represent human feelings and thoughts in their works. At least that is what Socrates, the great philosopher, tried to urge artists to do: "They should represent the activity of the 'soul', observing in detail the way in which 'feelings affect the body in action'."

Finally, they praised the beauty of the works and criticized how the form was generated. The main objective of Greek artists was beauty, dramatic expression, and harmony. It is no coincidence that Greece became the cradle of theater and philosophy, as interpretations and questioning were common activities in that place.

The Greeks left a very rich legacy in many ways. They explored, innovated, created, and represented themselves in every piece of their work. It was their looks and knowledge about each creation that came down to us. In this way, the creators are revealed in each work that we can admire today.

In addition to the aforementioned artists, other sculptors from the classical era also stood out, such as Praxiteles, Polycleto, and Lysippo.

ARCHITECTURE

We verified that the sculptures continued to be produced about or for the gods, since it is close to the temples or even inside them that they are found, in most cases. In this way, the importance of Greek architecture becomes clear; they are the owners of monuments classified as true sculptures. According to the characteristics of their columns, these styles can be divided into three types: Doric, Ionic, and Corinthian.

The expression "Doric order" refers to the components of the Doric temple, typical of mainland Greece. Many classify it as the most rustic of the three. The "Ionic order" was more widespread in the Greek settlements of Asia Minor and the Aegean and is basically characterized by its ornate capitals. The "Corinthian order" has columns topped with acanthus leaves. This latter developed much later and was not widely used outdoors until Roman times.

The curve along the top lines of a column was called entasis. Complying with the Greeks' fixation on harmony, this slight curve conveyed a more fluid effect, not a rigid one. Sometimes fluted columns were replaced by female figures called caryatids.

A mural in Pompeii presents some of the characteristics of Greek paintings of the time

PAINTINGS IN POMPEII

Access to ancient Greek paintings can also be gained through the murals and mosaics discovered in Pompeii, a small Roman city that was covered up when Mount Vesuvius erupted in 79 AC. There, almost all the houses and villages had wall paintings, illustrated colonnades and galleries, imitations of framed pictures, and theatrical stage sets. The artists, with great Hellenic influence, drew and painted freely using some techniques of perspective and light and shadow effects that they already mastered. In these paintings, it was found rural scenes, still life, landscapes – which was a great innovation –, and scenes with animals, among others.

PAINTING

Those who think that the revolution in art was just about sculptures are wrong. Greek painters also dared to use their techniques and observations. They were even more famous than the sculptors of that period. The negative fact is that no original works of Greek painting remained. Even so, through domestic ceramic objects, it is possible to have knowledge of the details of this art. Most of the objects found are Greek vases. They served as reservoirs for olive oil and wine, the main products of Ancient Greece.

Through the paintings on the vases, stories of gods and heroes of mythology were told, or contemporary events were narrated, such as festivals and wars. The oldest style of painting is geometric, which took its name from the shape of its figures and ornaments.

The Late Archaic Period was the apogee of painting on ceramic pieces. In the black-figure style adopted at the end of that time, the images were highlighted in black while the background was reddish. The artist scratched the details of the drawing with a needle and thus exposed the shade of clay. The red-figure style, which emerged around 530 BC, reversed the color scheme.

THEATER IN ANCIENT GREECE

The consolidation process of theater in Ancient Greece occurred as a result of manifestations in honor of Dionysus, the god of wine. With each new harvest of grapes, there was a great festivity to thank the god through processions.

Over time, these processions, called "dithyrambs," became increasingly elaborate, and, thus, choir directors emerged. The participants presented scenes about the adventures of Dionysus, sang,

Aeschylus, the father of Greek tragedy, would have died tragically

AESCHYLUS AND HIS BIZARRE DEATH

The story of the death of Aeschylus, the father of tragedy, is considered extremely bizarre. It is said that he was the victim of his own baldness. He would have died when a hungry eagle dropped a tortoise on his head so that the shell would break, and the bird would have access to the meat. Apparently, the eagle mistook Aeschylus' bald head for a rock.

and danced. Usually, around 20,000 people gathered in urban areas.

The first choir director was Thespis, invited by the tyrant Pisistratus to direct the procession in Athens. Thespis developed the use of masks to represent characters. Due to the large number of participants, it was impossible for everyone to listen to the reports, but they could visualize the feeling of the scene through the masks. The choir was composed of the narrators of the story, who, through representation, songs, and dances, told the stories of the character. He was the intermediary between the actor and the audience, and brought thoughts and feelings to the surface, in addition to also presenting the conclusion of the play.

There was also the Coryphaeus, a representative of the choir who communicated with the audience. In one of these processions, Thespis innovated by coming up onto a platform to respond to the choir and thus became the first choir responder. As a result, dialogue emerged, and Thespis became the first Greek actor.

Comedy in Ancient Greece was based on political satire. Aristophanes (448 to 380 BC) is considered the greatest representative of ancient comedy and the only author whose complete works are still preserved today. There is also an almost complete comedy of Menander. The three great masters of Greek tragedy were Aeschylus, Sophocles, and Euripides. Aeschylus (525 to 456 BC) has Prometheus Bound as his main text, which tells facts about the gods and myths. Sophocles (496 to 406 BC) is the author of the famous Oedipus Rex, a character in Greek mythology and also a tragedy written around 427 BC. Euripides (484 to 406 BC) had as his main contribution the work "The Trojan Women."

HOMERIC NARRATIVES INFLUENCE EDUCATION

The poems "Iliad" – which deals with the war between Greeks and Trojans – and "Odyssey" – a narrative about the return home of one of the Greek heroes who fought in Troy –, had direct importance in the formation of the Greek man.

Athenians, Thebans, and Spartans had an aristocratic education, that is, people were educated based on the model of the heroes of Homeric stories in order to imitate their virtues and become better citizens. Among these qualities were courage, prudence, and cunning.

Homer's narratives, when read in groups, guaranteed students a greater ability to understand the classical Greek language and the rhythm of the verses. This made it easier to communicate in all activities.

MUSIC

The Greeks are also responsible for laying the foundations for the musical culture of the West. In the cities of Tiryns, Mycenae, and Knossos, music was performed in an integrated way with poetry and dance. The poems were recited to the musical accompaniment of the lyre, which originated the use of the term "lyric" for this poetic genre. The most important instruments, besides the lyre, were the zither and the aulos (wind).

The development of music parallel to the development of Greek cities gave rise to philosophical theories that sought to understand its meaning and importance. Plato considered that music had great power of influence over man, so it should be under the control of the State, considered responsible for guaranteeing the social good.